THE YALE SHAKESPEARE

EDITED BY

WILBUR L. CROSS   TUCKER BROOKE

PUBLISHED UNDER THE DIRECTION
OF THE
DEPARTMENT OF ENGLISH, YALE UNIVERSITY,
ON THE FUND
GIVEN TO THE YALE UNIVERSITY PRESS IN 1917
BY THE MEMBERS OF THE
KINGSLEY TRUST ASSOCIATION
TO COMMEMORATE THE SEVENTY-FIFTH ANNIVERSARY
OF THE FOUNDING OF THE SOCIETY

·: *The Yale Shakespeare* :·

THE MERRY WIVES OF WINDSOR

EDITED BY

GEORGE VAN SANTVOORD

NEW HAVEN AND LONDON · YALE UNIVERSITY PRESS

Printed in the United States
of America

TABLE OF CONTENTS

Parte of Creſwells walke

[DRAMATIS PERSONÆ

SIR JOHN FALSTAFF
FENTON, *a young Gentleman*
SHALLOW, *a Country Justice*
SLENDER, *Cousin to Shallow*
FORD ⎫
PAGE ⎭ *two Gentlemen dwelling at Windsor*
WILLIAM PAGE, *a Boy, Son to Page*
SIR HUGH EVANS, *a Welsh Parson*
DOCTOR CAIUS, *a French Physician*
HOST *of the Garter Inn*
BARDOLPH ⎫
PISTOL ⎬ *Followers of Falstaff*
NYM ⎭
ROBIN, *Page to Falstaff*
SIMPLE, *Servant to Slender*
RUGBY, *Servant to Doctor Caius*

MISTRESS FORD
MISTRESS PAGE
ANNE PAGE, *her Daughter, in love with Fenton*
MISTRESS QUICKLY, *Servant to Doctor Caius*

Servants to Page, Ford, &c.

SCENE: *Windsor; and the Neighbourhood.*]

Dramatis Personæ: *first given by Rowe (1709)*

The Merry Wives of Windsor

ACT FIRST

Scene One

[Windsor.   Before Page's House]

***Enter** Justice Shallow, Slender, [and] Sir Hugh
Evans; [and later] Master Page, Falstaff, Bar-
dolph, Nym, Pistol, Anne Page, Mistress Ford,
Mistress Page, [and] Simple.*

Shal. Sir Hugh, persuade me not; I will
make a Star-chamber matter of it; if he were
twenty Sir John Falstaffs he shall not abuse
Robert Shallow, esquire.   4

Slen. In the county of Gloucester, justice of
peace, and *coram.*

Shal. Ay, cousin Slender, and *cust-alorum.*

Slen. Ay, and *rato-lorum* too; and a gentle- 8
man born, Master Parson; who writes himself
armigero, in any bill, warrant, quittance, or
obligation,—*armigero.*

Shal. Ay, that I do; and have done any time 12
these three hundred years.

Slen. All his successors gone before him hath
done 't; and all his ancestors that come after him
may: they may give the dozen white luces in 16
their coat.

Shal. It is an old coat.

Scene One S. d.; *cf. n.*   Sir: *old title for a priest*
2 Star-chamber matter; *cf. n.*   6 coram; *cf. n.*
7, 8 cust-alorum . . . rato-lorum; *cf. n.*
10 armigero: *esquire*   bill: *bill of exchange*   quittance: *discharge
    from debt*   16 give: *display*   luces: *pikes (fish)*; *cf. n.*

Eva. The dozen white louses do become an old coat well; it agrees well, *passant;* it is a 20 familiar beast to man, and signifies love.

Shal. The luce is the fresh fish; the salt fish is an old coat.

Slen. I may quarter, coz?   24

Shal. You may, by marrying.

Eva. It is marring indeed, if he quarter it.

Shal. Not a whit.

Eva. Yes, py'r lady; if he has a quarter of 28 your coat, there is but three skirts for yourself, in my simple conjectures: but that is all one. If Sir John Falstaff have committed disparagements unto you, I am of the Church, and will be 32 glad to do my benevolence to make atonements and compremises between you.

Shal. The Council shall hear it; it is a riot.

Eva. It is not meet the Council hear a riot; 36 there is no fear of Got in a riot. The Council, look you, shall desire to hear the fear of Got, and not to hear a riot; take your vizaments in that.

Shal. Ha! o' my life, if I were young again, 40 the sword should end it.

Eva. It is petter that friends is the sword, and end it; and there is also another device in my prain, which, peradventure, prings goot dis- 44 cretions with it. There is Anne Page, which is daughter to Master Thomas Page, which is pretty virginity.

Slen. Mistress Anne Page? She has brown 48 hair, and speaks small like a woman.

---

20 passant: *walking (heraldry)*   22, 23 *Cf. n.*
24 quarter; *cf. n.*   34 compremises: *i.e., compromises*
35 Council: *i.e., the Privy Council sitting in Star Chamber*
39 vizaments: *i.e., avisements, deliberations*
48 Mistress: *formal title for women*   49 small: *shrilly*

Eva. It is that fery person for all the 'orld, as just as you will desire; and seven hundred pounds of moneys, and gold and silver, is her grandsire, 52 upon his death's-bed,—Got deliver to a joyful resurrections!—give, when she is able to overtake seventeen years old. It were a goot motion if we leave our pribbles and prabbles, and desire a 56 marriage between Master Abraham and Mistress Anne Page.

Shal. Did her grandsire leave her seven hundred pound?　　　　　　　　　　60

Eva. Ay, and her father is make her a petter penny.

Shal. I know the young gentlewoman; she has good gifts.　　　　　　　　　　64

Eva. Seven hundred pounds and possibilities is goot gifts.

Shal. Well, let us see honest Master Page. Is Falstaff there?　　　　　　　　　　68

Eva. Shall I tell you a lie? I do despise a liar as I do despise one that is false; or as I despise one that is not true. The knight, Sir John, is there; and, I beseech you, be ruled by 72 your well-willers. I will peat the door for Master Page. [*Knocks.*] What, hoa! Got pless your house here!

Page. [*Within.*] Who's there?　　　　76

Eva. Here is Got's plessing, and your friend, and Justice Shallow; and here young Master Slender, that peradventures shall tell you another tale, if matters grow to your likings.　　80

---

50 'orld: *i.e., world*
56 pribbles and prabbles: *quibbles and brabbles* (?), *i.e., petty disputings*　　　　　　64 gifts: *qualities of mind*
65 possibilities: *expectations*

[Enter Page.]

Page. I am glad to see your worships well. I thank you for my venison, Master Shallow.

Shal. Master Page, I am glad to see you: much good do it your good heart! I wished your venison better; it was ill killed. How doth good Mistress Page?—and I thank you always with my heart, la! with my heart. 84

Page. Sir, I thank you. 88

Shal. Sir, I thank you; by yea and no, I do.

Page. I am glad to see you, good Master Slender.

Slen. How does your fallow greyhound, sir? I heard say he was outrun on Cotsall. 92

Page. It could not be judged, sir.

Slen. You'll not confess, you'll not confess.

Shal. That he will not: 'tis your fault, 'tis your fault. 'Tis a good dog. 96

Page. A cur, sir.

Shal. Sir, he's a good dog, and a fair dog; can there be more said? he is good and fair. Is Sir John Falstaff here? 100

Page. Sir, he is within; and I would I could do a good office between you.

Eva. It is spoke as a Christians ought to speak.

Shal. He hath wronged me, Master Page. 105

Page. Sir, he doth in some sort confess it.

Shal. If it be confessed, it is not redressed: is not that so, Master Page? He hath wronged me; indeed, he hath;—at a word, he hath,—believe me: Robert Shallow, esquire, saith, he is wronged. 108

Page. Here comes Sir John. 112

92 fallow: *fawn-color*   93 Cotsall; *cf. n.*
96 fault: *misfortune*

[*Enter Sir John Falstaff, Pistol, Bardolph, and Nym.*]

Fal. Now, Master Shallow, you'll complain of me to the king?

Shal. Knight, you have beaten my men, killed my deer, and broke open my lodge.　　　116

Fal. But not kissed your keeper's daughter?

Shal. Tut, a pin! this shall be answered.

Fal. I will answer it straight: I have done all this. That is now answered.　　　120

Shal. The Council shall know this.

Fal. 'Twere better for you if it were known in counsel: you'll be laughed at.

Eva. Pauca verba, Sir John; goot worts.　　124

Fal. Good worts! good cabbage. Slender, I broke your head: what matter have you against me?

Slen. Marry, sir, I have matter in my head 128 against you; and against your cony-catching rascals, Bardolph, Nym, and Pistol. [They carried me to the tavern, and made me drunk, and afterwards picked my pocket.]　　　132

Bard. You Banbury cheese!

Slen. Ay, it is no matter.

Pist. How now, Mephistophilus!

Slen. Ay, it is no matter.　　　136

Nym. Slice, I say! pauca, pauca; slice! that's my humour.

Slen. Where's Simple, my man? can you tell, cousin?　　　140

---

118 pin: *trifle*　　　answered: *atoned for*
119 straight: *immediately*　　　123 in counsel: *in secret*
124 Pauca verba: *few words*　　worts: *i.e., words*
125 worts: *vegetables*　　　129 cony-catching: *cheating*
130-132 They . . . pocket; *cf. n.*　　133 Banbury cheese; *cf. n.*
135 Mephistophilus: *devil; cf. n.*　　137 Slice: *of cheese (?): cf. n.*
138 humour; *cf. n.*

Eva. Peace, I pray you. Now let us understand: there is three umpires in this matter, as
I understand; that is—Master Page, *fidelicet,*
Master Page; and there is myself, *fidelicet,* my- 144
self; and the three party is, lastly and finally,
mine host of the Garter.

Page. We three, to hear it and end it between
them.   148

Eva. Fery goot: I will make a prief of it in
my note-book; and we will afterwards 'ork upon
the cause with as great discreetly as we can.

Fal. Pistol!   152

Pist. He hears with ears.

Eva. The tevil and his tam! what phrase is
this, 'He hears with ear'? Why, it is affectations.

Fal. Pistol, did you pick Master Slender's 156
purse?

Slen. Ay, by these gloves, did he,—or I would
I might never come in mine own great chamber
again else,—of seven groats in mill-sixpences, 160
and two Edward shovel-boards, that cost me two
shilling and two pence a-piece of Yead Miller, by
these gloves.

Fal. Is this true, Pistol?   164

Eva. No; it is false, if it is a pick-purse.

Pist. Ha, thou mountain foreigner!—Sir John and
    master mine,
I combat challenge of this latten bilbo.
Word of denial in thy labras here!   168

143 fidelicet: *i.e., videlicet, namely*
146 Garter: *an inn at Windsor*   159 great chamber: *hall*
160 groats: *coins valued at fourpence*   mill-sixpences: *coins with*
    raised borders   *raised borders*
161 Edward shovel-boards: *broad shillings; cf. n.*
162 Yead: *abbreviation of Edward*
166 mountain foreigner: *Welshman*
167 latten bilbo: *brass sword*
                                               168 labras: *lips*

Word of denial: froth and scum, thou liest.

Slen. By these gloves, then, 'twas he.

Nym. Be avised, sir, and pass good humours.
I will say, 'marry trap,' with you, if you run the 172
nuthook's humour on me: that is the very note
of it.

Slen. By this hat, then, he in the red face had
it; for though I cannot remember what I did 176
when you made me drunk, yet I am not altogether an ass.

Fal. What say you, Scarlet and John?   179

Bard. Why, sir, for my part, I say, the gentleman had drunk himself out of his five sentences.

Eva. It is his 'five senses'; fie, what the ignorance is!

Bard. And being fap, sir, was, as they say, 184
cashier'd; and so conclusions pass'd the careires.

Slen. Ay, you spake in Latin then too; but
'tis no matter. I'll ne'er be drunk whilst I live
again, but in honest, civil, godly company, for 188
this trick: if I be drunk, I'll be drunk with those
that have tne fear of God, and not with drunken
knaves.

Eva. So Got udge me, that is a virtuous mind. 192

Fal. You hear all these matters denied, gentlemen; you hear it.

[*Enter Anne Page with wine; Mistress Ford and
Mistress Page following.*]

Page. Nay, daughter, carry the wine in; we'll
drink within.   [*Exit Anne Page.*] 196

171 avised: *advised*   172 marry trap: *be off with you* (?)
172, 173 run . . . humour; *cf. n.*   173 very note: *exact information*
179 Scarlet and John; *cf. n.*   184 fap: *drunk*
185 cashier'd: *slang for robbed*   careires; *cf. n.*
192 udge: *i.e., judge*

Slen. O heaven! this is Mistress Anne Page.

Page. How now, Mistress Ford!

Fal. Mistress Ford, by my troth, you are very well met: by your leave, good mistress.   200

[*Kisses her.*]

Page. Wife, bid these gentlemen welcome. Come, we have a hot venison pasty to dinner: come, gentlemen, I hope we shall drink down all unkindness.   204

[*Exeunt all except Shallow,
Slender, and Evans.*]

Slen. I had rather than forty shillings I had my Book of Songs and Sonnets here.

[*Enter Simple.*]

How now, Simple! Where have you been? I must wait on myself, must I? You have not the 208 Book of Riddles about you, have you?

Sim. Book of Riddles! why, did you not lend it to Alice Shortcake upon All-Hallowmas last, a fortnight afore Michaelmas?   212

Shal. Come, coz; come, coz; we stay for you. A word with you, coz; marry, this, coz: there is, as 'twere a tender, a kind of tender, made afar off by Sir Hugh here: do you understand me?   216

Slen. Ay, sir, you shall find me reasonable: if it be so, I shall do that that is reason.

Shal. Nay, but understand me.

Slen. So I do, sir.   220

Eva. Give ear to his motions, Master Slender: I will description the matter to you, if you pe capacity of it.

206 Book of Songs and Sonnets; *cf. n.*
211 All-Hallowmas: *All Saints' Day, November 1*
212 Michaelmas: *St. Michael's Day, September 29*
213 stay: *wait*   215 tender: *offer*   afar off: *indirectly*

Slen. Nay, I will do as my cousin Shallow 226 says. I pray you pardon me; he's a justice of peace in his country, simple though I stand here.

Eva. But that is not the question; the question is concerning your marriage.   **228**

Shal. Ay, there's the point, sir.

Eva. Marry, is it, the very point of it; to Mistress Anne Page.

Slen. Why, if it be so, I will marry her upon 232 any reasonable demands.

Eva. But can you affection the 'oman? Let us command to know that of your mouth or of your lips; for divers philosophers hold that 236 the lips is parcel of the mouth: therefore, precisely, can you carry your good will to the maid?

Shal. Cousin Abraham Slender, can you love 240 her?

Slen. I hope, sir, I will do as it shall become one that would do reason.

Eva. Nay, Got's lords and his ladies! you 244 must speak possitable, if you can carry her your desires towards her.

Shal. That you must. Will you, upon good dowry, marry her?   **248**

Slen. I will do a greater thing than that, upon your request, cousin, in any reason.

Shal. Nay, conceive me, conceive me, sweet coz: what I do, is to pleasure you, coz. Can you 252 love the maid?

Slen. I will marry her, sir, at your request; but if there be no great love in the beginning,

226 simple though: *as sure as*   237 parcel: *part*
245 possitable: *i.e., positively*   251 conceive: *understand*
252 pleasure: *please*

yet heaven may decrease it upon better ac- 256
quaintance, when we are married and have more
occasion to know one another: I hope, upon
familiarity will grow more contempt: but if you
say, 'Marry her,' I will marry her; that I am 260
freely dissolved, and dissolutely.

Eva. It is a fery discretion answer; save, the
faul is in the 'ort 'dissolutely': the 'ort is, according to our meaning, 'resolutely.' His mean- 264
ing is goot.

Shal. Ay, I think my cousin meant well.

Slen. Ay, or else I would I might be hanged,
la! 268

Shal. Here comes fair Mistress Anne.

[*Enter Anne Page.*]

Would I were young for your sake, Mistress
Anne.

Anne. The dinner is on the table; my father 272
desires your worships' company.

Shal. I will wait on him, fair Mistress Anne.

Eva. Od's plessed will! I will not be absence
at the grace.   [*Exeunt Shallow and Evans.*] 276

Anne. Will 't please your worship to come
in, sir?

Slen. No, I thank you, forsooth, heartily; I
am very well. 280

Anne. The dinner attends you, sir.

Slen. I am not a-hungry, I thank you forsooth. Go, sirrah, for all you are my man, go
wait upon my cousin Shallow. [*Exit Simple.*] A 284
justice of peace sometime may be beholding to
his friend for a man. I keep but three men and

263 faul: *i.e., fault*   'ort: *i.e., word*   275 Od's: *i.e., God's*
281 attends: *awaits*   283 sirrah: *fellow*

a boy yet, till my mother be dead; but what
though? yet I live like a poor gentleman 288
born.

Anne. I may not go in without your worship:
they will not sit till you come.

Slen. I' faith, I'll eat nothing; I thank you 292
as much as though I did.

Anne. I pray you, sir, walk in.

Slen. I had rather walk here, I thank you. I
bruised my shin th' other day with playing at 296
sword and dagger with a master of fence; three
veneys for a dish of stewed prunes;—and, by my
troth, I cannot abide the smell of hot meat
since. Why do your dogs bark so? be there 300
bears i' the town?

Anne. I think there are, sir; I heard them
talked of.

Slen. I love the sport well; but I shall as 304
soon quarrel at it as any man in England.
You are afraid, if you see the bear loose, are
you not?

Anne. Ay, indeed, sir.   308

Slen. That's meat and drink to me, now: I
have seen Sackerson loose twenty times, and
have taken him by the chain; but, I warrant
you, the women have so cried and shrieked at 312
it, that it passed: but women, indeed, cannot
abide 'em; they are very ill-favoured rough
things.

[Enter Page.]

Page. Come, gentle Master Slender, come; 316
we stay for you.

297 fence: *fencing*
304 the sport: *i.e., bear-baiting*
313 passed: *beat everything*
298 veneys: *fencing-bouts*
310 Sackerson; *cf. n.*
314 ill-favoured: *ugly*

Slen. I'll eat nothing, I thank you, sir.

Page. By cock and pie, you shall not choose, sir! come, come.   320

Slen. Nay, pray you, lead the way.

Page. Come on, sir.

Slen. Mistress Anne, yourself shall go first.

Anne. Not I, sir; pray you, keep on.   324

Slen. Truly, I will not go first: truly, la! I will not do you that wrong.

Anne. I pray you, sir.

Slen. I'll rather be unmannerly than trouble- 328 some. You do yourself wrong, indeed, la! *Exeunt.*

Scene Two

[*The Same*]

Enter Evans and Simple.

Eva. Go your ways, and ask of Doctor Caius' house, which is the way: and there dwells one Mistress Quickly, which is in the manner of his nurse, or his try nurse, or his cook, or his laun- 4 dry, his washer, and his wringer.

Sim. Well, sir.

Eva. Nay, it is petter yet. Give her this let- ter; for it is a 'oman that altogether's ac- 8 quaintance with Mistress Anne Page: and the letter is, to desire and require her to solicit your master's desires to Mistress Anne Page. I pray you, be gone: I will make an end of my 12 dinner; there's pippins and seese to come.

Exeunt.

319 By cock and pye: *a petty oath*   3 manner: *capacity*
13 seese: *i.e., cheese*

Scene Three

[A Room in the Garter Inn]

Enter Falstaff, Host, Bardolph, Nym, Pistol, [and] Page [Robin].

Fal. Mine host of the Garter!

Host. What says my bully-rook? Speak scholarly and wisely.

Fal. Truly, mine host, I must turn away 4 some of my followers.

Host. Discard, bully Hercules; cashier: let them wag; trot, trot.

Fal. I sit at ten pounds a week. 8

Host. Thou'rt an emperor, Cæsar, Keisar, and Pheezar. I will entertain Bardolph; he shall draw, he shall tap: said I well, bully Hector?

Fal. Do so, good mine host. 12

Host. I have spoke; let him follow. *[To Bardolph.]* Let me see thee froth and lime: I am at a word; follow. *[Exit.]*

Fal. Bardolph, follow him. A tapster is a 16 good trade: an old cloak makes a new jerkin; a withered serving-man, a fresh tapster. Go; adieu.

Bard. It is a life that I have desired. I will thrive. 20

Pist. O base Hungarian wight! wilt thou the spigot wield? *[Exit Bardolph.]*

Nym. He was gotten in drink; is not the humour conceited? 24

---

2 bully-rook: *fine fellow (slang)*
8 I sit at: *my expenses are*
10 entertain: *employ as servant*
11 draw: *draw liquor*   tap: *act as tapster*
14 froth and lime; *cf. n.*
17 jerkin: *jacket*
23 gotten: *begotten*

7 wag: *go their way*
9, 10 Keisar, and Pheezar; *cf. n.*
14, 15 at a word: *ready*
21 wight: *man; cf. n.*
24 conceited: *ingenious*

Fal. I am glad I am so acquit of this tinder-box; his thefts were too open; his filching was like an unskilful singer; he kept not time.

Nym. The good humour is to steal at a minim's rest. 28

Pist. 'Convey,' the wise it call. 'Steal!' foh! a fico for the phrase!

Fal. Well, sirs, I am almost out at heels. 32

Pist. Why, then, let kibes ensue.

Fal. There is no remedy; I must cony-catch, I must shift.

Pist. Young ravens must have food. 36

Fal. Which of you know Ford of this town?

Pist. I ken the wight: he is of substance good.

Fal. My honest lads, I will tell you what I am about. 40

Pist. Two yards, and more.

Fal. No quips now, Pistol! Indeed, I am in the waist two yards about; but I am now about no waste; I am about thrift. Briefly, I do mean to make love to Ford's wife: I spy entertainment in her; she discourses, she carves, she gives the leer of invitation: I can construe the action of her familiar style; and the hardest voice of her behaviour, to be Englished rightly, is, 'I am Sir John Falstaff's.' 44 48

Pist. He hath studied her well, and translated her well, out of honesty into English. 52

Nym. The anchor is deep: will that humour pass?

25 acquit: *rid*   29 minim's rest: *time of a half measure* (*music*)
30 Convey: *thieves' slang for steal*   31 fico: *fig*
32 out at heels: *out of money*   33 kibes: *chilblains*
35 shift: *devise a trick*   38 ken: *know*
47 carves: *shows courtesy*   48 action: *gesture*
53 honesty: *chastity*   54 anchor . . . deep; *cf. n.*

Fal. Now, the report goes she has all the rule 56
of her husband's purse; he hath a legion of
angels.

Pist. As many devils entertain, and 'To her,
boy,' say I.   60

Nym. The humour rises; it is good: humour
me the angels.

Fal. I have writ me here a letter to her; and
here another to Page's wife, who even now gave 64
me good eyes too, examined my parts with most
judicious œillades: sometimes the beam of her
view gilded my foot, sometimes my portly belly.

Pist. Then did the sun on dunghill shine.   68

Nym. I thank thee for that humour.

Fal. O! she did so course o'er my exteriors
with such a greedy intention, that the appetite
of her eye did seem to scorch me up like a burn- 72
ing-glass. Here's another letter to her: she
bears the purse too; she is a region in Guiana,
all gold and bounty. I will be 'cheator to them
both, and they shall be exchequers to me: they 76
shall be my East and West Indies, and I will
trade to them both. Go bear thou this letter to
Mistress Page; and thou this to Mistress Ford.
We will thrive, lads, we will thrive.   80

Pist. Shall I Sir Pandarus of Troy become,
And by my side wear steel? then, Lucifer take all!

Nym. I will run no base humour: here, take
the humour-letter. I will keep the haviour of 84
reputation.

Fal. [*To Robin.*] Hold, sirrah, bear you these
letters tightly:

5C angels. *gold coins valued at about half a sovereign.*
66 œillades: *amorous glances*
75 'cheator; *cf. n.*
84 haviour: *behavior*
                                      74 Guiana; *cf. n.*
                           81 Sir Pandarus; *cf. n*
                                86 tightly: *safely*

Sail like my pinnace to these golden shores.
Rogues, hence! avaunt! vanish like hailstones, go;   88
Trudge, plod away o' the hoof; seek shelter, pack!
Falstaff will learn the humour of this age,
French thrift, you rogues: myself and skirted page.
                              [*Exeunt Falstaff and Robin.*]

Pist. Let vultures gripe thy guts! for gourd and
    fullam holds,   92
And high and low beguile the rich and poor.
Tester I'll have in pouch when thou shalt lack,
Base Phrygian Turk!

Nym. I have operations [in my head,] which   96
be humours of revenge.

Pist. Wilt thou revenge?

Nym. By welkin and her star!

Pist. With wit or steel?   100

Nym. With both the humours, I:
I will discuss the humour of this love to Page.

Pist.   And I to Ford shall eke unfold
                How Falstaff, varlet vile,   104
             His dove will prove, his gold will hold,
                And his soft couch defile.

Nym. My humour shall not cool: I will
incense Page to deal with poison; I will possess   108
him with yellowness, for the revolt of mine is
dangerous: that is my true humour.

Pist. Thou art the Mars of malcontents: I
second thee; troop on.   [*Exeunt.*] 112

88 avaunt: *be off*   89 pack: *depart*
91 French thrift; *cf. n.*   skirted: *wearing a coat with skirts*
92 gourd and fullam; *cf. n.*
93 high and low: *i.e., high and low numbers on dice*
94 Tester: *sixpence*   pouch: *purse*   99 welkin: *sky*
102 discuss: *tell*   108 deal with: *employ*
108, 109 possess . . . yellowness: *make him jealous*
109 the revolt of mine: *i.e., my revolt*

Scene Four

[A Room in Doctor Caius's House]

***Enter Mistress Quickly, Simple, [and] John Rugby;
[and later] Doctor Caius, and Fenton.***

Quick. What, John Rugby!—
I pray thee, go to the casement, and see if you
can see my master, Master Doctor Caius, coming: if he do, i' faith, and find anybody in the 4
house, here will be an old abusing of God's
patience and the king's English.

Rug. I'll go watch.

Quick. Go: and we'll have a posset for 't soon 8
at night, in faith, at the latter end of a sea-coal
fire. *[Exit Rugby.]* An honest, willing, kind
fellow, as ever servant shall come in house
withal; and, I warrant you, no tell-tale, nor 12
no breed-bate: his worst fault is, that he is
given to prayer; he is something peevish that
way, but nobody but has his fault; but let that
pass. Peter Simple you say your name is? 16

Sim. Ay, for fault of a better.

Quick. And Master Slender's your master?

Sim. Ay, forsooth.

Quick. Does he not wear a great round beard 20
like a glover's paring-knife?

Sim. No, forsooth: he hath but a little whey-
face, with a little yellow beard—a Cain-coloured
beard. 24

Quick. A softly-sprighted man, is he not?

5 old: *great*   8 posset: *hot milk curdled with ale*
8, 9 soon at night: *as soon as night comes*
9 sea-coal: *mineral coal (i.e., not charcoal) brought by sea*
12 withal: *with*   13 breed-bate: *mischief-maker*
14 peevish: *silly*   17 fault: *lack*
23 Cain-coloured; *cf. n.*   25 softly-sprighted: *gentle (?)*

Sim. Ay, forsooth; but he is as tall a man of
his hands as any is between this and his head:
he hath fought with a warrener.   28

Quick. How say you?—O! I should remember
him: does he not hold up his head, as it were,
and strut in his gait?

Sim. Yes, indeed, does he.   32

Quick. Well, heaven send Anne Page no
worse fortune! Tell Master Parson Evans I will
do what I can for your master: Anne is a good
girl, and I wish—   36

[*Enter Rugby.*]

Rug. Out, alas! here comes my master.

Quick. We shall all be shent. Run in here,
good young man; go into this closet. He will not
stay long. [*Shuts Simple in the closet.*] What, 40
John Rugby! John, what, John, I say! Go, John,
go inquire for my master; I doubt he be not
well, that he comes not home. [*Exit Rugby.*]
[*Singing.*]

'And down, down, adown-a,' &c.   44

[*Enter Doctor Caius.*]

Caius. Vat is you sing? I do not like dese
toys. Pray you, go and vetch me in my closet
une boitine verde; a box, a green-a box: do intend vat I speak? a green-a box.   48

Quick. Ay, forsooth; I'll fetch it you. [*Aside.*]
I am glad he went not in himself: if he had found
the young man, he would have been horn-mad.

Caius. *Fe, fe, fe, fe! ma foi, il fait fort* 52

26 tall: *valiant*
38 shent: *scolded*   42 doubt: *fear*
47 intend: *hear (Fr. entendre)*
28 warrener: *gamekeeper*
46 toys: *foolish things*
51 horn-mad: *stark-mad*

chaud.   Je m'en vais à la cour,—la grande affaire.

Quick. Is it this, sir?

Caius. Oui; mettez le au mon pocket; *dé-* 56 *pêchez,* quickly.—Vere is dat knave Rugby?

Quick. What, John Rugby! John!

[*Enter Rugby.*]

Rug. Here, sir.

Caius. You are John Rugby, and you are 60 Jack Rugby: come, take-a your rapier, and come after my heel to de court.

Rug. 'Tis ready, sir, here in the porch.

Caius. By my trot, I tarry too long.—Od's 64 me! *Qu'ay j'oublié?* dere is some simples in my closet, dat I will not for de varld I shall leave behind.

Quick. [*Aside.*] Ay me! he'll find the young 68 man there, and be mad.

Caius. O diable! diable! vat is in my closet? —Villain! *larron!* [*Pulling Simple out.*] Rugby, my rapier!   72

Quick. Good master, be content.

Caius. Verefore shall I be content-a?

Quick. The young man is an honest man.

Caius. Vat shall de honest man do in my 76 closet? dere is no honest man dat shall come in my closet.

Quick. I beseech you, be not so phlegmatic. Hear the truth of it: he came of an errand to 80 me from Parson Hugh.

Caius. Vell.

Sim. Ay, forsooth, to desire her to—

---

64 trot: *troth*   65 simples: *medicinal herbs*
79 phlegmatic: *i.e., choleric* (?)

Quick. Peace, I pray you.   84

Caius. Peace-a your tongue!—Speak-a your tale.

Sim. To desire this honest gentlewoman, your maid, to speak a good word to Mistress Anne 88 Page for my master in the way of marriage.

Quick. This is all, indeed, la! but I'll ne'er put my finger in the fire, and need not.

Caius. Sir Hugh send-a you?—Rugby, *baillez* 92 me some paper: tarry you a little-a while. [*Writes.*]

Quick. [*Aside to Simple.*] I am glad he is so quiet: if he had been throughly moved, you should have heard him so loud, and so melancholy. 96 But, notwithstanding, man, I'll do your master what good I can; and the very yea and the no is, the French doctor, my master,—I may call him my master, look you, for I keep his house; and I 100 wash, wring, brew, bake, scour, dress meat and drink, make the beds, and do all myself,—

Sim. [*Aside to Quickly.*] 'Tis a great charge to come under one body's hand.   104

Quick. [*Aside to Simple.*] Are you avis'd o' that? you shall find it a great charge: and to be up early and down late; but notwithstanding,— to tell you in your ear,—I would have no words 108 of it,—my master himself is in love with Mistress Anne Page: but notwithstanding that, I know Anne's mind, that's neither here nor there.

Caius. You jack'nape, give-a dis letter to 112 Sir Hugh; by gar, it is a challenge: I vill cut his troat in de Park; and I vill teach a scurvy jack-a-nape priest to meddle or make. You may

92 baillez: *fetch*   95 throughly: *thoroughly*
103 charge: *burden*   112 jack'nape: *coxcomb*
115 meddle or make: *interfere*

be gone; it is not good you tarry here: by gar, 116
I vill cut all his two stones; by gar, he shall not
have a stone to trow at his dog.   [*Exit Simple.*]

Quick. Alas! he speaks but for his friend.

Caius. It is no matter-a for dat:—do not you 120
tell-a me dat I shall have Anne Page for myself?
By gar, I vill kill de Jack priest; and I have
appointed mine host of de *Jartiere* to measure our
weapon. By gar, I vill myself have Anne Page. 124

Quick. Sir, the maid loves you, and all shall
be well. We must give folks leave to prate:
what, the good-jer!

Caius. Rugby, come to the court vit me. By 128
gar, if I have not Anne Page, I shall turn your
head out of my door. Follow my heels, Rugby.
                    [*Exeunt Caius and Rugby.*]

Quick. You shall have An fool's-head of your
own. No, I know Anne's mind for that: never a 132
woman in Windsor knows more of Anne's mind
than I do; nor can do more than I do with her,
I thank heaven.

Fent. [*Within.*] Who's within there? ho!   136

Quick. Who's there, I trow? Come near the
house, I pray you.

[*Enter Fenton.*]

Fent. How now, good woman! how dost thou?

Quick. The better, that it pleases your good 140
worship to ask.

Fent. What news? how does pretty Mistress
Anne?

Quick. In truth, sir, and she is pretty, and 144

122 Jack: *term of contempt*
123, 124 measure our weapon: *i.e., as umpire in a duel*
127 good-jer: *an expression of disgust*   131 An fool's-head; *cf. n.*
137 trow: *wonder*   Come near: *enter*

honest, and gentle; and one that is your friend,
I can tell you that by the way; I praise heaven
for it.

Fent. Shall I do any good, thinkest thou? 148
Shall I not lose my suit?

Quick. Troth, sir, all is in his hands above;
but notwithstanding, Master Fenton, I'll be
sworn on a book, she loves you. Have not your 152
worship a wart above your eye?

Fent. Yes, marry have I; what of that?

Quick. Well, thereby hangs a tale. Good
faith, it is such another Nan; but, I detest, 156
an honest maid as ever broke bread: we had
an hour's talk of that wart. I shall never laugh
but in that maid's company;—but, indeed, she
is given too much to allicholy and musing. 160
But for you—well, go to.

Fent. Well, I shall see her to-day. Hold,
there's money for thee; let me have thy voice in
my behalf: if thou seest her before me, com- 164
mend me.

Quick. Will I? i' faith, that we will: and
I will tell your worship more of the wart the
next time we have confidence; and of other 168
wooers.

Fent. Well, farewell; I am in great haste now.

Quick. Farewell to your worship. [*Exit Fenton.*] Truly, an honest gentleman: but Anne 172
loves him not; for I know Anne's mind as well
as another does. Out upon 't! what have I
forgot?
                                              Exit.

145 honest: *chaste*   160 allicholy: *i.e., melancholy*
161 go to: *no more of that!*

ACT SECOND

Scene One

[*Before Page's House*]

Enter Mistress Page, [*with a letter; and later*] *Mistress Ford, Master Page, Master Ford, Pistol, Nym,* [*Mistress*] *Quickly, Host,* [*and*] *Shallow.*

Mrs. Page. What! have I 'scaped love-letters in the holiday-time of my beauty, and am I now a subject for them?   Let me see.   [*Reads.*]

'Ask me no reason why I love you; for though   4
Love use Reason for his physician, he admits him
not for his counsellor.   You are not young, no
more am I; go to then, there's sympathy; you
are merry, so am I; ha! ha! then, there's more   8
sympathy; you love sack, and so do I; would you
desire better sympathy?   Let it suffice thee, Mistress Page, at the least, if the love of a soldier can
suffice, that I love thee.   I will not say, pity me,— 12
'tis not a soldier-like phrase; but I say, love me.
By me,

            Thine own true knight,
            By day or night,   16
            Or any kind of light,
            With all his might
            For thee to fight,   JOHN FALSTAFF.'

What a Herod of Jewry is this!   O wicked, wicked 20
world! one that is well-nigh worn to pieces with
age, to show himself a young gallant!   What an
unweighed behaviour hath this Flemish drunk-

7 sympathy: *agreement*   9 sack: *white Spanish wine*
20 Herod of Jewry; *cf. n.*
23 unweighed: *inconsiderate*   Flemish drunkard; *cf. n.*

ard picked, with the devil's name! out of my 24
conversation, that he dares in this manner assay
me? Why, he hath not been thrice in my company! What should I say to him? I was then
frugal of my mirth:—heaven forgive me! Why, 28
I'll exhibit a bill in the parliament for the
putting down of men. How shall I be revenged
on him? for revenged I will be, as sure as his
guts are made of puddings.					32

[*Enter Mistress Ford.*]

Mrs. Ford. Mistress Page! trust me, I was
going to your house.

Mrs. Page. And, trust me, I was coming to
you. You look very ill.					36

Mrs. Ford. Nay, I'll ne'er believe that: I have
to show to the contrary.

Mrs. Page. Faith, but you do, in my mind.

Mrs. Ford. Well, I do then; yet, I say I could 40
show you to the contrary. O, Mistress Page!
give me some counsel.

Mrs. Page. What's the matter, woman?

Mrs. Ford. O woman, if it were not for one 44
trifling respect, I could come to such honour!

Mrs. Page. Hang the trifle, woman; take the
honour. What is it?—dispense with trifles;—
what is it?					48

Mrs. Ford. If I would but go to hell for an
eternal moment or so, I could be knighted.

Mrs. Page. What? thou liest. Sir Alice
Ford! These knights will hack; and so thou 52
shouldst not alter the article of thy gentry.

25 conversation: *conduct*					29 exhibit: *submit for consideration*
30 putting down: *destroying*
32 puddings: *stuffed intestines, sausages*
52 hack: *grow common* (?); *cf. n.*
53 article . . . gentry: *character of your rank*

Mrs. Ford. We burn daylight: here, read, read; perceive how I might be knighted. I shall think the worse of fat men as long as I 56 have an eye to make difference of men's liking: and yet he would not swear; praised women's modesty; and gave such orderly and well-behaved reproof to all uncomeliness, that I would have 60 sworn his disposition would have gone to the truth of his words; but they do no more adhere and keep place together than the Hundredth Psalm to the tune of 'Green Sleeves.' 64 What tempest, I trow, threw this whale, with so many tuns of oil in his belly, ashore at Windsor? How shall I be revenged on him? I think, the best way were to entertain him with hope, till the 68 wicked fire of lust have melted him in his own grease. Did you ever hear the like?

Mrs. Page. Letter for letter, but that the name of Page and Ford differs! To thy great 72 comfort in this mystery of ill opinions, here's the twin brother of thy letter: but let thine inherit first; for, I protest, mine never shall. I warrant, he hath a thousand of these letters, 76 writ with blank space for different names, sure more, and these are of the second edition. He will print them, out of doubt; for he cares not what he puts into the press, when he would put 80 us two: I had rather be a giantess, and lie under Mount Pelion. Well, I will find you twenty lascivious turtles ere one chaste man.

54 burn daylight: *waste time*
57 make difference: *discriminate between*   liking: *looks*
60 uncomeliness: *rude behavior*
61, 62 disposition . . . words; *cf. n.*   63 adhere: *agree*
64 Green Sleeves; *cf. n.*   68 entertain: *fill his thoughts*
83 turtles: *turtle doves, symbolic of faithful love*

Mrs. Ford. Why, this is the very same; the very 84
hand, the very words. What doth he think of us?

Mrs. Page. Nay, I know not: it makes me
almost ready to wrangle with mine own honesty.
I'll entertain myself like one that I am not 88
acquainted withal; for, sure, unless he know
some strain in me, that I know not myself, he
would never have boarded me in this fury.

Mrs. Ford. Boarding call you it? I'll be sure 92
to keep him above deck.

Mrs. Page. So will I: if he come under my
hatches, I'll never to sea again. Let's be revenged on him: let's appoint him a meeting; 96
give him a show of comfort in his suit, and lead
him on with a fine-baited delay, till he hath
pawned his horses to mine host of the Garter.

Mrs. Ford. Nay, I will consent to act any vil- 100
lainy against him, that may not sully the chariness of our honesty. O, that my husband saw this
letter! it would give eternal food to his jealousy.

Mrs. Page. Why, look where he comes; and 104
my good man too: he's as far from jealousy, as
I am from giving him cause; and that, I hope,
is an unmeasurable distance.

Mrs. Ford. You are the happier woman.   108

Mrs. Page. Let's consult together against
this greasy knight. Come hither.   [*They retire.*]

[*Enter Ford, with Pistol; and Page, with Nym.*]

Ford. Well, I hope it be not so.

Pist. Hope is a curtal dog in some affairs: 112
Sir John affects thy wife.

Ford. Why, sir, my wife is not young.

88 entertain: *treat*   98 fine-baited: *subtly alluring*
101 chariness: *scrupulous integrity*
112 curtal: *having tail docked*   113 affects: *is fond of*

Pist. He woos both high and low, both rich
and poor,

Both young and old, one with another, Ford.   116
He loves the galimaufry: Ford, perpend.

Ford. Love my wife!

Pist. With liver burning hot: prevent, or go
thou,

Like Sir Actæon he, with Ringwood at thy heels.— 120
O! odious is the name!

Ford. What name, sir?

Pist. The horn, I say. Farewell:

Take heed; have open eye, for thieves do foot by
night: 124

Take heed, ere summer comes or cuckoo-birds do
sing.

Away, sir Corporal Nym!

Believe it, Page; he speaks sense.   [*Exit.*]

Ford. [*Aside.*] I will be patient: I will find 128
out this.

Nym. [*To Page.*] And this is true; I like not
the humour of lying. He hath wronged me in
some humours: I should have borne the hu- 132
moured letter to her, but I have a sword and it
shall bite upon my necessity. He loves your
wife; there's the short and the long. My name
is Corporal Nym; I speak, and I avouch 'tis 136
true: my name is Nym, and Falstaff loves your
wife. Adieu. I love not the humour of bread
and cheese; [and there's the humour of it.]
Adieu.   [*Exit.*] 140

Page. 'The humour of it,' quoth 'a! here's
a fellow frights humour out of his wits.

117 galimaufry: *medley*   perpend: *consider*
119 liver: *supposed seat of love*
120 Actæon . . . Ringwood; *cf. n.*   124 foot: *walk*
125 cuckoo-birds; *cf. n.*

Ford. I will seek out Falstaff.

Page. I never heard such a drawling, affect- 144
ing rogue.

Ford. If I do find it: well.

Page. I will not believe such a Cataian,
though the priest o' the town commended him 148
for a true man.

Ford. 'Twas a good sensible fellow; well.

Page. How now, Meg!

[*Mrs. Page and Mrs. Ford come forward.*]

Mrs. Page. Whither go you, George?—Hark 152
you.

Mrs. Ford. How now, sweet Frank! why art
thou melancholy?

Ford. I melancholy! I am not melancholy. 156
Get you home, go.

Mrs. Ford. Faith, thou hast some crotchets
in thy head now. Will you go, Mistress Page?

Mrs. Page. Have with you. You'll come to 160
dinner, George? [*Aside to Mrs. Ford.*] Look,
who comes yonder: she shall be our messenger
to this paltry knight.

Mrs. Ford. [*Aside to Mrs. Page.*] Trust me, 164
I thought on her: she'll fit it.

[*Enter Mistress Quickly.*]

Mrs. Page. You are come to see my daughter
Anne?

Quick. Ay, forsooth; and, I pray, how does 168
good Mistress Anne?

Mrs. Page. Go in with us, and see: we'd have
an hour's talk with you.

144 affecting: *affected*   147 Cataian: *Chinese; cf. n.*
158 crotchets: *whims*   160 Have with you: *I'll go along with you*

> [*Exeunt Mrs. Page, Mrs. Ford,*
> *and Mrs. Quickly.*]

Page. How now, Master Ford!   172

Ford. You heard what this knave told me, did you not?

Page. Yes; and you heard what the other told me?   176

Ford. Do you think there is truth in them?

Page. Hang 'em, slaves! I do not think the knight would offer it: but these that accuse him in his intent towards our wives, are a yoke of his 180 discarded men; very rogues, now they be out of service.

Ford. Were they his men?

Page. Marry, were they.   184

Ford. I like it never the better for that. Does he lie at the Garter?

Page. Ay, marry, does he. If he should intend this voyage towards my wife, I would 188 turn her loose to him; and what he gets more of her than sharp words, let it lie on my head.

Ford. I do not misdoubt my wife, but I would be loth to turn them together. A man 192 may be too confident: I would have nothing 'lie on my head': I cannot be thus satisfied.

Page. Look, where my ranting host of the Garter comes. There is either liquor in his 19⟨6⟩ pate or money in his purse when he looks so merrily.—

[*Enter Host.*]

How now, mine host!

Host. How now, bully-rook! thou'rt a gentle- 200 man. Cavaliero-justice, I say!

---

180 yoke: *pair*   181 very: *thorough*
191 misdoubt: *mistrust*   201 Cavaliero-justice; *cf. n.*

[Enter Shallow.]

Shal. I follow, mine host, I follow. Good even
and twenty, good Master Page! Master Page, will
you go with us? we have sport in hand.   204

Host. Tell him, cavaliero-justice; tell him,
bully-rook.

Shal. Sir, there is a fray to be fought between
Sir Hugh the Welsh priest and Caius the French 208
doctor.

Ford. Good mine host o' the Garter, a word
with you.   *[Drawing him aside.]*

Host. What sayest thou, my bully-rook?   212

Shal. *[To Page.]* Will you go with us to
behold it? My merry host hath had the measur-
ing of their weapons, and, I think, hath appointed them contrary places; for, believe me, I 216
hear the parson is no jester. Hark, I will tell
you what our sport shall be. *[They converse apart.]*

Host. Hast thou no suit against my knight,
my guest-cavalier?   220

Ford. None, I protest: but I'll give you a
pottle of burnt sack to give me recourse to him
and tell him my name is Brook, only for a jest.

Host. My hand, bully: thou shalt have egress 224
and regress; said I well? and thy name shall be
Brook. It is a merry knight. Will you go,
mynheers?

Shal. Have with you, mine host.   228

Page. I have heard, the Frenchman hath
good skill in his rapier.

Shal. Tut, sir! I could have told you more.
In these times you stand on distance, your 232

202, 203 Good even and twenty; *cf. n.*   216 contrary: *different*
222 pottle: *tankard*   burnt sack: *warm wine*   recourse: *access*
227 mynheers: *sirs*   232 distance: *interval between fencers*

passes, stoccadoes, and I know not what: 'tis
the heart, Master Page; 'tis here, 'tis here. I
have seen the time with my long sword I would
have made you four tall fellows skip like rats. 236

Host. Here, boys, here, here! shall we wag?

Page. Have with you. I had rather hear
them scold than fight.

[*Exeunt Host, Shallow, and Page.*]

Ford. Though Page be a secure fool, and 240
stands so firmly on his wife's frailty, yet I cannot
put off my opinion so easily. She was in his
company at Page's house, and what they made
there, I know not. Well, I will look further 244
into 't; and I have a disguise to sound Falstaff.
If I find her honest, I lose not my labour; if she
be otherwise, 'tis labour well bestowed.   [*Exit.*]

Scene Two

[*A Room in the Garter Inn*]

Enter Falstaff [*and*] *Pistol;* [*and later*] *Robin,* [*Mistress*] *Quickly, Bardolph,* [*and*] *Ford.*

Fal. I will not lend thee a penny.

Pist. Why, then the world's mine oyster,
Which I with sword will open.
[I will retort the sum in equipage.]   4

Fal. Not a penny. I have been content, sir,
you should lay my countenance to pawn: I have
grated upon my good friends for three reprieves
for you and your coach-fellow Nym; or else you 8

233 passes: *lunges*   stoccadoes: *thrusts*
236 made you: *made ('you' is 'ethical')*   240 secure: *unsuspicious*
4 retort: *i.e., repay*   equipage; *cf. n.*
6 countenance; *cf. n.*   8 coach-fellow: *mate*

had looked through the grate, like a geminy of
baboons. I am damned in hell for swearing to
gentlemen my friends, you were good soldiers
and tall fellows; and when Mistress Bridget lost 12
the handle of her fan, I took 't upon mine honour
thou hadst it not.

Pist. Didst thou not share? hadst thou not fifteen
pence?

Fal. Reason, you rogue, reason: thinkest 16
thou, I'll endanger my soul gratis? At a word,
hang no more about me; I am no gibbet for you:
go: a short knife and a throng!—to your manor
of Pickt-hatch! go. You'll not bear a letter for 20
me, you rogue!—you stand upon your honour!—
Why, thou unconfinable baseness, it is as much
as I can do to keep the terms of mine honour
precise. I, I, I, myself sometimes, leaving the 24
fear of God on the left hand and hiding mine
honour in my necessity, am fain to shuffle, to
hedge and to lurch; and yet you, rogue, will
ensconce your rags, your cat-a-mountain looks, 28
your red-lattice phrases, and your bold-beating
oaths, under the shelter of your honour! You
will not do it, you!

Pist. I do relent: what wouldst thou more of
man?   32

[*Enter Robin.*]

Rob. Sir, here's a woman would speak with
you.

Fal. Let her approach.

[*Enter Mistress Quickly.*]

9 geminy: *pair*   13 handle; *cf. n.*   took 't: *swore*
19 short knife: *for cutting purses*   20 Pickt-hatch; *cf. n.*
26 shuffle: *equivocate*   27 hedge: *cheat*   lurch: *lie in ambush*
28 cat-a-mountain: *wildcat*
29 red-lattice phrases: *alehouse talk*   bold-beating: *blustering*

Quick. Give your worship good morrow.   36
Fal. Good morrow, good wife.
Quick. Not so, an 't please your worship.
Fal. Good maid, then.
Quick. I'll be sworn   40
As my mother was, the first hour I was born.
Fal. I do believe the swearer. What with me?
Quick. Shall I vouchsafe your worship a word
or two?   44
Fal. Two thousand, fair woman; and I'll
vouchsafe thee the hearing.
Quick. There is one Mistress Ford, sir,—I
pray, come a little nearer this ways:—I myself 48
dwell with Master Doctor Caius.
Fal. Well, on: Mistress Ford, you say,—
Quick. Your worship says very true:—I pray
your worship, come a little nearer this ways.   52
Fal. I warrant thee, nobody hears; mine own
people, mine own people.
Quick. Are they so? God bless them, and
make them his servants!   56
Fal. Well: Mistress Ford; what of her?
Quick. Why, sir, she's a good creature. Lord,
Lord! your worship's a wanton! Well, heaven
forgive you, and all of us, I pray!   60
Fal. Mistress Ford; come, Mistress Ford,—
Quick. Marry, this is the short and the long
of it. You have brought her into such a canaries
as 'tis wonderful: the best courtier of them all, 64
when the court lay at Windsor, could never have
brought her to such a canary; yet there has been
knights, and lords, and gentlemen, with their
coaches, I warrant you, coach after coach, letter 68
after letter, gift after gift; smelling so sweetly—

3 canaries: *i.e., quandary* (?)

all musk, and so rushling, I warrant you, in silk
and gold; and in such alligant terms; and in
such wine and sugar of the best and the fairest, 72
that would have won any woman's heart; and, I
warrant you, they could never get an eye-wink of
her. I had myself twenty angels given me this
morning; but I defy all angels, in any such sort, 76
as they say, but in the way of honesty: and, I
warrant you, they could never get her so much
as sip on a cup with the proudest of them all;
and yet there has been earls, nay, which is more, 80
pensioners; but, I warrant you, all is one with her.

Fal. But what says she to me? be brief, my
good she-Mercury.

Quick. Marry, she hath received your letter; 84
for the which she thanks you a thousand times;
and she gives you to notify that her husband
will be absence from his house between ten and
eleven.   88

Fal. Ten and eleven?

Quick. Ay, forsooth; and then you may come
and see the picture, she says, that you wot of:
Master Ford, her husband, will be from home. 92
Alas! the sweet woman leads an ill life with him;
he's a very jealousy man; she leads a very
frampold life with him, good heart.

Fal. Ten and eleven. Woman, commend me 96
to her; I will not fail her.

Quick. Why, you say well. But I have another messenger to your worship: Mistress Page
hath her hearty commendations to you too: 100
and let me tell you in your ear, she's as fartuous

---

70 rushling: *i.e., rustling*   71 alligant: *i.e., eloquent*
81 pensioners: *gentlemen of the sovereign's bodyguard*
83 she-Mercury: *female messenger*
95 frampold: *quarrelsome*   91 wot: *know*
                                                   101 fartuous: *i.e., virtuous*

a civil modest wife, and one, I tell you, that will
not miss you morning nor evening prayer, as any
is in Windsor, whoe'er be the other: and she 104
bade me tell your worship that her husband is
seldom from home; but, she hopes there will
come a time. I never knew a woman so dote
upon a man: surely, I think you have charms, 108
la; yes, in truth.

Fal. Not I, I assure thee: setting the attraction
of my good parts aside, I have no other charms.

Quick. Blessing on your heart for 't! 112

Fal. But, I pray thee, tell me this: has Ford's
wife and Page's wife acquainted each other how
they love me?

Quick. That were a jest indeed! they have 116
not so little grace, I hope: that were a trick,
indeed! But Mistress Page would desire you to
send her your little page, of all loves: her husband has a marvellous infection to the little 120
page; and, truly, Master Page is an honest man.
Never a wife in Windsor leads a better life than
she does: do what she will, say what she will,
take all, pay all, go to bed when she list, rise 124
when she list, all is as she will: and, truly she
deserves it; for if there be a kind woman in
Windsor, she is one. You must send her your
page; no remedy. 128

Fal. Why, I will.

Quick. Nay, but do so, then: and, look you,
he may come and go between you both; and in
any case have a nay-word, that you may know 132
one another's mind, and the boy never need to

111 parts: *qualities*
120 infection: *i.e., affection*
132 nay-word: *password*

119 of all loves: *for love's sake*
124 list: *please*

understand anything; for 'tis not good that
children should know any wickedness: old folks,
you know, have discretion, as they say, and 136
know the world.

Fal. Fare thee well: commend me to them
both. There's my purse; I am yet thy debtor.—
Boy, go along with this woman.—[*Exeunt Mis-* 140
tress Quickly and Robin.] This news distracts
me.

Pist. This punk is one of Cupid's carriers.
Clap on more sails; pursue; up with your fights; 144
Give fire! she is my prize, or ocean whelm them all!
                                                    [*Exit.*]

Fal. Sayest thou so, old Jack? go thy ways;
I'll make more of thy old body than I have done.
Will they yet look after thee? Wilt thou, after 148
the expense of so much money, be now a gainer?
Good body, I thank thee. Let them say 'tis
grossly done; so it be fairly done, no matter.

[*Enter Bardolph.*]

Bard. Sir John, there's one Master Brook 152
below would fain speak with you, and be acquainted with you: and hath sent your worship
a morning's draught of sack.

Fal. Brook is his name?   156
Bard. Ay, sir.
Fal. Call him in. [*Exit Bardolph.*] Such
Brooks are welcome to me, that o'erflow such
liquor. Ah, ha! Mistress Ford and Mistress 160
Page, have I encompassed you? go to; *via!*

[*Enter Bardolph, with Ford, disguised.*]

---

143 punk: *strumpet*   carriers: *messengers*   144 fights; *cf. n.*
145 my prize; *cf. n.*   151 grossly: *heavily*
159 Brooks; *cf. n.*   161 encompassed: *outwitted*   via: *go on*

Ford. Bless you, sir!

Fal. And you, sir; would you speak with me?

Ford. I make bold to press with so little preparation upon you.　　　　　　　　　　　165

Fal. You're welcome. What's your will?—
Give us leave, drawer.　　　　　　　*[Exit Bardolph.]*

Ford. Sir, I am a gentleman that have spent 168
much: my name is Brook.

Fal. Good Master Brook, I desire more acquaintance of you.

Ford. Good Sir John, I sue for yours: not to 172
charge you; for I must let you understand I
think myself in better plight for a lender than
you are: the which hath something emboldened
me to this unseasoned intrusion; for, they say, 176
if money go before, all ways do lie open.

Fal. Money is a good soldier, sir, and will
on.

Ford. Troth, and I have a bag of money here 180
troubles me: if you will help to bear it, Sir
John, take all, or half, for easing me of the car-
riage.

Fal. Sir, I know not how I may deserve to be 184
your porter.

Ford. I will tell you, sir, if you will give me
the hearing.

Fal. Speak, good Master Brook; I shall be 188
glad to be your servant.

Ford. Sir, I hear you are a scholar,—I will be
brief with you, and you have been a man long
known to me, though I had never so good means, 192
as desire, to make myself acquainted with you.
I shall discover a thing to you, wherein I must

---

167 Give us leave: *withdraw*　　173 charge: *cause expense to*
176 unseasoned: *ill-timed*　　　194 discover: *disclose*

very much lay open mine own imperfection; but,
good Sir John, as you have one eye upon my 196
follies, as you hear them unfolded, turn another
into the register of your own, that I may pass
with a reproof the easier, sith you yourself know
how easy it is to be such an offender.   200

Fal. Very well, sir; proceed.

Ford. There is a gentlewoman in this town,
her husband's name is Ford.

Fal. Well, sir.   204

Ford. I have long loved her, and, I protest
to you, bestowed much on her; followed her
with a doting observance; engrossed opportunities to meet her; fee'd every slight occasion 208
that could but niggardly give me sight of her;
not only bought many presents to give her, but
have given largely to many to know what she
would have given. Briefly, I have pursued her 212
as love hath pursued me; which hath been on
the wing of all occasions. But whatsoever I have
merited, either in my mind or in my means,
meed, I am sure, I have received none; unless 216
experience be a jewel that I have purchased at
an infinite rate; and that hath taught me to
say this,

'Love like a shadow flies when substance love pursues;   220
Pursuing that that flies, and flying what pursues.'

Fal. Have you received no promise of satis-
faction at her hands?

Ford. Never.   224

198 register: *record*   199 sith: *since*
207 engrossed: *bought up wholesale*   208 fee'd: *employed*
220, 221 Cf. *n.*

Fal. Have you importuned her to such a purpose?

Ford. Never.

Fal. Of what quality was your love, then? 228

Ford. Like a fair house built upon another man's ground; so that I have lost my edifice by mistaking the place where I erected it.

Fal. To what purpose have you unfolded this 232 to me?

Ford. When I have told you that, I have told you all. Some say, that though she appear honest to me, yet in other places she enlargeth her 236 mirth so far that there is shrewd construction made of her. Now, Sir John, here is the heart of my purpose: you are a gentleman of excellent breeding, admirable discourse, of great ad- 240 mittance, authentic in your place and person, generally allowed for your many warlike, court-like, and learned preparations.

Fal. O, sir! 244

Ford. Believe it, for you know it. There is money; spend it, spend it; spend more; spend all I have; only give me so much of your time in exchange of it, as to lay an amiable siege to 248 the honesty of this Ford's wife: use your art of wooing, win her to consent to you; if any man may, you may as soon as any.

Fal. Would it apply well to the vehemency 252 of your affection, that I should win what you would enjoy? Methinks you prescribe to yourself very preposterously.

Ford. O, understand my drift. She dwells so 256

237 shrewd: *evil*   240 admittance: *fashion*
241 authentic: *powerful*   242 allowed: *approved*
243 preparations: *accomplishments*   248 amiable: *amorous*

securely on the excellency of her honour, that
the folly of my soul dares not present itself: she
is too bright to be looked against. Now, could I
come to her with any detection in my hand, my 260
desires had instance and argument to commend
themselves: I could drive her then from the ward
of her purity, her reputation, her marriage-vow,
and a thousand other her defences, which now 264
are too-too strongly embattled against me.
What say you to 't, Sir John?

Fal. Master Brook, I will first make bold with
your money; next, give me your hand; and 268
last, as I am a gentleman, you shall, if you will,
enjoy Ford's wife.

Ford. O good sir!

Fal. I say you shall.   272

Ford. Want no money, Sir John; you shall
want none.

Fal. Want no Mistress Ford, Master Brook;
you shall want none. I shall be with her, I may 276
tell you, by her own appointment; even as you
came in to me, her assistant or go-between
parted from me: I say I shall be with her between ten and eleven; for at that time the jeal- 280
ous rascally knave her husband will be forth.
Come you to me at night; you shall know how I
speed.

Ford. I am blest in your acquaintance. Do 284
you know Ford, sir?

Fal. Hang him, poor cuckoldly knave! I
know him not. Yet I wrong him, to call him
poor: they say the jealous wittolly knave hath 288

261 instance: *evidence*   262 ward: *posture of defence (fencing)*
281 forth: *away from home*
286 cuckoldly: *having an unfaithful wife*   288 wittolly: *cuckoldly*

masses of money; for the which his wife seems
to me well-favoured. I will use her as the key of
the cuckoldly rogue's coffer; and there's my
harvest-home.　　　　　　　　　　　292

Ford. I would you knew Ford, sir, that you
might avoid him, if you saw him.

Fal. Hang him, mechanical salt-butter rogue!
I will stare him out of his wits; I will awe him 296
with my cudgel·it shall hang like a meteor o'er
the cuckold's horns. Master Brook, thou shalt
know I will predominate over the peasant, and
thou shalt lie with his wife. Come to me soon at 300
night. Ford's a knave, and I will aggravate his
style; thou, Master Brook, shalt know him for
knave and cuckold. Come to me soon at night.
　　　　　　　　　　　　　　　[*Exit.*]

Ford. What a damned Epicurean rascal is 304
this! My heart is ready to crack with impatience.
Who says this is improvident jealousy? my wife
hath sent to him, the hour is fixed, the match is
made. Would any man have thought this? See 308
the hell of having a false woman! My bed shall
be abused, my coffers ransacked, my reputation
gnawn at; and I shall not only receive this
villainous wrong, but stand under the adoption 312
of abominable terms, and by him that does me
this wrong. Terms! names! Amaimon sounds
well; Lucifer, well; Barbason, well; yet they
are devils' additions, the names of fiends: but 316
Cuckold! Wittol!—Cuckold! the devil himself

290 well-favoured: *good-looking*
295 mechanical: *vulgar*　　　salt-butter: *rank* (?)
299 predominate: *have ascendancy*
301 aggravate: *add to*　　　　　　　　　　302 style: *title*
304 Epicurean: *sensual*　　　312, 313 stand . . . terms; *cf. n.*
314, 315 Amaimon, Barbason: *devils*
316 additions: *titles*　　　　　　　317 Wittol: *contented cuckold*

hath not such a name. Page is an ass, a secure
ass: he will trust his wife; he will not be jealous.
I will rather trust a Fleming with my butter, 320
Parson Hugh the Welshman with my cheese, an
Irishman with my aqua-vitæ bottle, or a thief to
walk my ambling gelding, than my wife with herself: then she plots, then she ruminates, then she 324
devises; and what they think in their hearts
they may effect, they will break their hearts but
they will effect. God be praised for my jealousy! Eleven o'clock the hour: I will prevent 328
this, detect my wife, be revenged on Falstaff, and
laugh at Page. I will about it; better three
hours too soon than a minute too late. Fie, fie,
fie! cuckold! cuckold! cuckold!   *Exit.* 332

Scene Three

[*A Field near Windsor*]

Enter Caius [and] Rugby; [and later] Page, Shal-
low, Slender, [and] Host.

Caius. Jack Rugby!
Rug. Sir?
Caius. Vat is de clock, Jack?
Rug. 'Tis past the hour, sir, that Sir Hugh 4
promised to meet.
Caius. By gar, he has save his soul, dat he is
no come: he has pray his Pible vell, dat he is no
come. By gar, Jack Rugby, he is dead already, 8
if he be come.
Rug. He is wise, sir; he knew your worship
would kill him, if he came.
Caius. By gar, de herring is no dead so as I 12

vill kill him.   Take your rapier, Jack; I vill tell
you how I vill kill him.

Rug. Alas, sir! I cannot fence.

Caius. Villainy, take your rapier.   16

Rug. Forbear; here's company.

[*Enter Host, Shallow, Slender, and Page.*]

Host. Bless thee, bully Doctor!

Shal. Save you, Master Doctor Caius!

Page. Now, good Master Doctor!   20

Slen. Give you good morrow, sir.

Caius. Vat be all you, one, two, tree, four,
come for?

Host. To see thee fight, to see thee foin, to 24
see thee traverse; to see thee here, to see thee
there; to see thee pass thy punto, thy stock, thy
reverse, thy distance, thy montant.   Is he dead,
my Ethiopian? is he dead, my Francisco? ha, 28
bully! What says my Æsculapius? my Galen?
my heart of elder? ha! is he dead, bully stale?
is he dead?

Caius. By gar, he is de coward Jack priest of 32
de vorld; he is not show his face.

Host. Thou art a Castilian King Urinal!
Hector of Greece, my boy!

Caius. I pray you, bear vitness that me have 36
stay six or seven, two, tree hours for him, and
he is no come.

Shal. He is the wiser man, Master Doctor:
he is a curer of souls, and you a curer of 40

---

24 foin: *thrust (fencing)*   25 traverse: *march back and forth*
26, 27 punto . . . montant: *fencing terms; cf. n.*
28 Francisco: *i.e., Frenchman*
29 Æsculapius: *Greek god of medicine*   Galen: *Greek physician
of second century A. D.*
30 heart of elder: *coward; cf. n.*   stale; *cf. n.*
35 Hector of Greece: *i.e., valiant warrior*

bodies; if you should fight, you go against the
hair of your professions. Is it not true, Master
Page?

Page. Master Shallow, you have yourself been 44
a great fighter, though now a man of peace.

Shal. Bodykins, Master Page, though I now
be old and of the peace, if I see a sword out, my
finger itches to make one. Though we are jus- 48
tices and doctors and churchmen, Master Page,
we have some salt of our youth in us; we are
the sons of women, Master Page.

Page. 'Tis true, Master Shallow.   52

Shal. It will be found so, Master Page. Master Doctor Caius, I am come to fetch you home.
I am sworn of the peace: you have showed
yourself a wise physician, and Sir Hugh hath 56
shown himself a wise and patient churchman.
You must go with me, Master Doctor.

Host. Pardon, guest-justice.—A word, Mon-
sieur Mockwater.   60

Caius. Mock-vater! vat is dat?

Host. Mock-water, in our English tongue, is
valour, bully.

Caius. By gar, den, I have as mush mock- 64
vater as de Englishman.—Scurvy jack-dog
priest! by gar, me vill cut his ears.

Host. He will clapper-claw thee tightly, bully.

Caius. Clapper-de-claw! vat is dat?   68

Host. That is, he will make thee amends.

Caius. By gar, me do look, he shall clapper-
de-claw me; for, by gar, me vill have it.

42 hair: *grain*   46 Bodykins: *God's body*
48 make one: *join in*   50 salt: *quality*
60 Mockwater: *physician (slang)*   67 clapper-claw: *thrash*

Host. And I will provoke him to 't, or let him 72
wag.

Caius. Me tank you for dat.

Host. And moreover, bully,—But first, Master
guest, and Master Page, and eke Cavaliero Slen- 76
der, go you through the town to Frogmore.

                                              [*Aside to them.*]

Page. Sir Hugh is there, is he?

Host. He is there: see what humour he is in;
and I will bring the doctor about by the fields. 80
Will it do well?

Shal. We will do it.

Page, Shal., and Slen. Adieu, good Master
Doctor.   [*Exeunt Page, Shallow, and Slender.*] 84

Caius. By gar, me vill kill de priest; for he
speak for a jack-an-ape to Anne Page.

Host. Let him die. Sheathe thy impatience;
throw cold water on thy choler: go about the 88
fields with me through Frogmore: I will bring
thee where Mistress Anne Page is, at a farm-
house a-feasting; and thou shalt woo her. Cried
game; said I well?   92

Caius. By gar, me tank you for dat: by gar,
I love you; and I shall procure-a you de good
guest, de earl, de knight, de lords, de gentlemen,
my patients.   96

Host. For the which I will be thy adversary
toward Anne Page: said I well?

Caius. By gar, 'tis good; vell said.

Host. Let us wag, then.   100

Caius. Come at my heels, Jack Rugby. *Exeunt.*

77 Frogmore; *cf. n.*   91, 92 Cried game; *cf. n.*

ACT THIRD

Scene One

[A Field near Frogmore]

Enter Evans [and] Simple; [and later] Page, Shallow, Slender, Host, Caius, [and] Rugby.

Eva. I pray you now, good Master Slender's serving-man, and friend Simple by your name, which way have you looked for Master Caius, that calls himself doctor of physic?   4

Sim. Marry, sir, the pittie-ward, the park-ward, every way; old Windsor way, and every way but the town way.

Eva. I most fehemently desire you you will   8
also look that way.

Sim. I will, sir.   *[Exit.]*

Eva. Pless my soul! how full of chollors I am, and trempling of mind! I shall be glad if he   12
have deceived me. How melancholies I am! I will knog his urinals about his knave's costard when I have goot opportunities for the 'ork: pless my soul!   *[Sings.]* 16

'To shallow rivers, to whose falls
    Melodious birds sing madrigals;
There will we make our peds of roses,
And a thousand fragrant posies.   20
        To shallow—'

Mercy on me! I have a great dispositions to cry.
                                    [Sings.]

---

5 pittie-ward: *toward the little park; cf. n.*
11 chollors: *choler, i.e., anger*
14 knog: *knock*   costard: *apple, used jokingly for head*
15 'ork: *i.e., work*
                                    17-26 *Cf. n.*

Melodious birds sing madrigals,—
When as I sat in Pabylon,—   24
And a thousand vagram posies.
    To shallow,—'

[*Enter Simple.*]

Sim. Yonder he is coming, this way, Sir Hugh.
Eva. He's welcome.   [*Sings.*] 28

'To shallow rivers, to whose falls—'

Heaven prosper the right!—what weapons is he?
Sim. No weapons, sir. There comes my
master, Master Shallow, and another gentleman, 32
from Frogmore, over the stile, this way.
Eva. Pray you, give me my gown; or else
keep it in your arms.   [*Reads in a book.*]

[*Enter Page, Shallow, and Slender.*]

Shal. How now, Master Parson! Good 36
morrow, good Sir Hugh. Keep a gamester from
the dice, and a good student from his book, and
it is wonderful.
Slen. [*Aside.*] Ah, sweet Anne Page!   40
Page. Save you, good Sir Hugh!
Eva. Pless you from His mercy sake, all of
you!
Shal. What, the sword and the word! do 44
you study them both, Master Parson?
Page. And youthful still in your doublet
and hose! this raw rheumatic day?
Eva. There is reasons and causes for it.   48
Page. We are come to you to do a good
office, Master Parson.
Eva. Fery well: what is it?

25 vagram: *i.e., fragrant*   46, 47 doublet and hose; *cf.* n.

Page. Yonder is a most reverend gentleman, 52 who, belike having received wrong by some person, is at most odds with his own gravity and patience that ever you saw.

Shal. I have lived fourscore years and up- 56 ward; I never heard a man of his place, gravity, and learning, so wide of his own respect.

Eva. What is he?

Page. I think you know him; Master Doctor 60 Caius, the renowned French physician.

Eva. Got's will, and his passion of my heart! I had as lief you would tell me of a mess of porridge.   64

Page. Why?

Eva. He has no more knowledge in Hibbocrates and Galen,—and he is a knave besides; a cowardly knave as you would desires to be 68 acquainted withal.

Page. I warrant you, he's the man should fight with him.

Slen. [*Aside.*] O, sweet Anne Page!   72

Shal. It appears so, by his weapons. Keep them asunder: here comes Doctor Caius.

[*Enter Host, Caius, and Rugby.*]

Page. Nay, good Master Parson, keep in your weapon.   76

Shal. So do you, good Master Doctor.

Host. Disarm them, and let them question: let them keep their limbs whole and hack our English.   80

Caius. I pray you, let-a me speak a word vit your ear: verefore vill you not meet-a me?

54 odds: *strife*   58 so . . . respect: *so indifferent to his reputation*
56 Hibbocrates: *i.e., Hippocrates, Greek physician and writer of fifth century B. C.*   78 question: *talk*

Eva. [*Aside to Caius.*] Pray you, use your
patience: in good time.   84

Caius. By gar, you are de coward, de Jack
dog, John ape.

Eva. [*Aside to Caius.*] Pray you, let us not
be laughing-stogs to other men's humours; I 88
desire you in friendship, and I will one way or
other make you amends. [*Aloud.*] I will knog
your urinals about your knave's cogscomb [for
missing your meetings and appointments.]   92

Caius. Diable!—Jack Rugby,—mine host de
Jarretierre,—have I not stay for him to kill
him? have I not, at de place I did appoint?

Eva. As I am a Christians soul, now, look you, 96
this is the place appointed: I'll be judgment by
mine host of the Garter.

Host. Peace, I say, Gallia and Gaul; French
and Welsh, soul-curer and body-curer!   100

Caius. Ay, dat is very good; excellent.

Host. Peace, I say! hear mine host of the
Garter. Am I politic? am I subtle? am I a
Machiavel? Shall I lose my doctor? no; he 104
gives me the potions and the motions. Shall I
lose my parson, my priest, my Sir Hugh? no;
he gives me the proverbs and the no-verbs. [Give
me thy hand, terrestrial; so;]—give me thy hand 108
celestial; so. Boys of art, I have deceived you
both, I have directed you to wrong places:
your hearts are mighty, your skins are whole,
and let burnt sack be the issue. Come, lay their 112
swords to pawn. Follow me, lads of peace;
follow, follow, follow.

99 Gallia: *i.e., Wales* (Fr. Galles)   104 Machiavel: *intriguer*
109 art: *learning*   112 issue: *conclusion*

Shal. Trust me, a mad host!—Follow, gentlemen, follow.   116

Slen. [*Aside.*] O, sweet Anne Page!

[*Exeunt Shallow, Slender, Page, and Host.*]

Caius. Ha! do I perceive dat? have you
make-a de sot of us, ha, ha?

Eva. This is well; he has made us his vlout- 120
ing-stog. I desire you that we may be friends
and let us knog our prains together to be revenge
on this same scall, scurvy, cogging companion,
the host of the Garter.   124

Caius. By gar, vit all my heart. He promise
to bring me vere is Anne Page: by gar, he
deceive me too.

Eva. Well, I will smite his noddles. Pray 128
you, follow.   [*Exeunt.*]

Scene Two

[*A Street in Windsor*]

[*Enter*] Mist[*ress*] *Page* [*and*] *Robin;* [*and later*]
    Ford, Page, Shallow, Slender, Host, Evans,
    [*and*] *Caius.*

Mrs. Page. Nay, keep your way, little gallant:
you were wont to be a follower, but now you
are a leader. Whether had you rather lead
mine eyes, or eye your master's heels?   4

Rob. I had rather, forsooth, go before you
like a man than follow him like a dwarf.

Mrs. Page. O! you are a flattering boy: now
I see you'll be a courtier.   8

---

119 sot: *fool*   120 vlouting-stog: *i.e., floutingstock, laughingstock*
123 scall: *i. e., scald, scurvy*   cogging: *cheating*
3 Whether: *(I wonder) whether*

[*Enter Ford.*]

Ford. Well met, Mistress Page. Whither go
you?

Mrs. Page. Truly, sir, to see your wife: is
she at home?   12

Ford. Ay; and as idle as she may hang together, for want of company. I think. if your
husbands were dead, you two would marry.

Mrs. Page. Be sure of that,—two other 16
husbands.

Ford. Where had you this pretty weather-
cock?

Mrs. Page. I cannot tell what the dickens 20
his name is my husband had him of. What do
you call your knight's name, sirrah?

Rob. Sir John Falstaff.

Ford. Sir John Falstaff!   24

Mrs. Page. He, he; I can never hit on's
name. There is such a league between my good
man and he! Is your wife at home indeed?

Ford. Indeed she is.   28

Mrs. Page. By your leave, sir: I am sick till
I see her.   [*Exeunt Mistress Page and Robin.*]

Ford. Has Page any brains? hath he any
eyes? hath he any thinking? Sure, they sleep; 32
he hath no use of them. Why, this boy will
carry a letter twenty mile, as easy as a cannon
will shoot point-blank twelve score. He pieces
out his wife's inclination; he gives her folly 36
motion and advantage: and now she's going to
my wife, and Falstaff's boy with her. A man may
hear this shower sing in the wind: and Fal-

26 league: *friendship*   35, 36 pieces out: *ekes out*
3? motion: *instigation*
39 hear . . . wind: *i.e., the matter is perfectly obvious*

staff's boy with her! Good plots! they are laid; 46
and our revolted wives share damnation together. Well; I will take him, then torture my
wife, pluck the borrowed veil of modesty from
the so seeming Mistress Page, divulge Page him- 44
self for a secure and wilful Actæon; and to
these violent proceedings all my neighbours
shall cry aim. [*Clock strikes.*] The clock gives
me my cue, and my assurance bids me search; 48
there I shall find Falstaff. I shall be rather
praised for this than mocked; for it is as posi-
tive as the earth is firm, that Falstaff is there:
I will go.   52

[*Enter Page, Shallow, Slender, Host, Sir Hugh
        Evans, Caius, and Rugby.*]

Shal., Page, &c. Well met, Master Ford.

Ford. Trust me, a good knot. I have good
cheer at home; and I pray you all go with me.

Shal. I must excuse myself, Master Ford.   50

Slen. And so must I, sir: we have appointed to
dine with Mistress Anne, and I would not break
with her for more money than I'll speak of.

Shal. We have lingered about a match be- 60
tween Anne Page and my cousin Slender, and
this day we shall have our answer.

Slen. I hope I have your good will, father
Page.   64

Page. You have, Master Slender; I stand
wholly for you: but my wife, Master Doctor, is
for you altogether.

Caius. Ay, by gar; and de maid is love-a me: 68
my nursh-a Quickly tell me so mush.

47 cry aim: *express their approval; cf. n.*   54 knot: *company*

Host. What say you to young Master Fenton?
he capers, he dances, he has eyes of youth, he
writes verses, he speaks holiday, he smells April 72
and May: he will carry 't, he will carry 't; 'tis in
his buttons; he will carry 't.

Page. Not by my consent, I promise you. The
gentleman is of no having: he kept company 76
with the wild prince and Poins; he is of too
high a region; he knows too much. No, he
shall not knit a knot in his fortunes with the
finger of my substance: if he take her, let him 80
take her simply; the wealth I have waits on my
consent, and my consent goes not that way.

Ford. I beseech you heartily, some of you go
home with me to dinner: besides your cheer, you 84
shall have sport; I will show you a monster.
Master Doctor, you shall go; so shall you,
Master Page; and you, Sir Hugh.

Shal. Well, fare you well: we shall have the 88
freer wooing at Master Page's.

        [Exeunt Shallow and Slender.]

Caius. Go home, John Rugby; I come anon.

        [Exit Rugby.]

Host. Farewell, my hearts: I will to my
honest knight Falstaff, and drink canary with 92
him.   *[Exit.]*

Ford. *[Aside.]* I think I shall drink in pipe-
wine first with him; I'll make him dance. Will
you go, gentles?   96

All. Have with you to see this monster.

        Exeunt.

72 holiday: *in choice language*
73, 74 he will . . . buttons: *he'll win; he has it in him*
76 having: *property*   77 prince and Poins; *cf. n.*
78 region: *height in the heavens*   81 simply: *by herself*
92 canary: *a sweet wine*   94 pipe-wine: *wine in the cask: cf. n.*

Scene Three

[A Room in Ford's House]

Enter M[*istress*] *Ford* [*and*] M[*istress*] *Page;* [*and later*] *Servants, Robin, Falstaff, Ford, Page, Caius,* [*and*] *Evans.*

Mrs. Ford. What, John! what, Robert!

Mrs. Page. Quickly, quickly:—Is the buck-basket—

Mrs. Ford. I warrant. What, Robin, I say!   4

[Enter Servants with a basket.]

Mrs. Page. Come, come, come.

Mrs. Ford. Here, set it down.

Mrs. Page. Give your men the charge; we must be brief.   8

Mrs. Ford. Marry, as I told you before, John, and Robert, be ready here hard by in the brew-house; and when I suddenly call you, come forth, and without any pause or staggering, take 12 this basket on your shoulders: that done, trudge with it in all haste, and carry it among the whitsters in Datchet-mead, and there empty it in the muddy ditch, close by the Thames side.   16

Mrs. Page. You will do it?

Mrs Ford. I have told them over and over; they lack no direction. Be gone, and come when you are called.   *[Exeunt Servants.]* 20

Mrs. Page. Here comes little Robin.

[Enter Robin.]

2 buck-basket: *basket for soiled linen*   7 charge: *order*
15 whitsters: *bleachers of linen*   Datchet-mead; *cf. n.*

Mrs. Ford. How now, my eyas-musket! what
news with you?

Rob. My master, Sir John, is come in at your 24
back-door, Mistress Ford, and requests your
company.

Mrs. Page. You little Jack-a-Lent, have you
been true to us? 28

Rob. Ay, I'll be sworn. My master knows not
of your being here, and hath threatened to put
me into everlasting liberty if I tell you of it; for
he swears he'll turn me away. 32

Mrs. Page. Thou'rt a good boy; this secrecy
of thine shall be a tailor to thee and shall make
thee a new doublet and hose. I'll go hide me.

Mrs. Ford. Do so. Go tell thy master I am 36
alone. [*Exit Robin.*] Mistress Page, remember
you your cue.

Mrs. Page. I warrant thee; if I do not act it,
hiss me. [*Exit.*] 40

Mrs. Ford. Go to, then: we'll use this
unwholesome humidity, this gross watery
pumpion; we'll teach him to know turtles
from jays. 44

[*Enter Falstaff.*]

Fal. 'Have I caught my heavenly jewel?'
Why, now let me die, for I have lived long
enough: this is the period of my ambition: O
this blessed hour! 48

Mrs. Ford. O, sweet Sir John!

Fal. Mistress Ford, I cannot cog, I cannot
prate, Mistress Ford. Now shall I sin in my

22 eyas-musket: *young sparrow-hawk*
27 Jack-a-Lent: *puppet used as target in a game*
43 pumpion: *pumpkin*   45 *Cf. n.*
47 period: *final point*   50 cog: *fawn*

wish: I would thy husband were dead. I'll 52
speak it before the best lord, I would make thee
my lady.

Mrs. Ford. I your lady, Sir John! alas, I
should be a pitiful lady.   56

Fal. Let the court of France show me such
another. I see how thine eye would emulate
the diamond: thou hast the right arched beauty
of the brow that becomes the ship-tire, the tire- 60
valiant, or any tire of Venetian admittance.

Mrs. Ford. A plain kerchief, Sir John: my
brows become nothing else; nor that well
neither.   64

Fal. By the Lord, thou art a traitor to say
so: thou wouldst make an absolute courtier;
and the firm fixture of thy foot would give an
excellent motion to thy gait in a semi-circled 68
farthingale. I see what thou wert, if Fortune
thy foe were not, Nature thy friend. Come,
thou canst not hide it.

Mrs. Ford. Believe me, there's no such thing 72
in me.

Fal. What made me love thee? let that persuade thee there's something extraordinary in
thee. Come, I cannot cog and say thou art this 76
and that, like a many of these lisping hawthorn-
buds, that come like women in men's apparel,
and smell like Bucklersbury in simple-time;
I cannot; but I love thee; none but thee; and 80
thou deservest it.

60 ship-tire: *headdress shaped like a ship*   tire-valiant: *fantastic*
    headdress   66 absolute: *perfect*
68, 69 semi-circled farthingale: *petticoat, the hoops of which did not*
    come round in front   69, 70 Fortune thy foe; *cf. n.*
77 hawthorn-buds: *dandies*   79 Bucklersbury; *cf. n.*

Mrs. Ford. Do not betray me, sir. I fear you
love Mistress Page.

Fal. Thou mightst as well say, I love to walk 84
by the Counter-gate, which is as hateful to me as
the reek of a lime-kiln.

Mrs. Ford. Well, heaven knows how I love
you; and you shall one day find it.   88

Fal. Keep in that mind; I'll deserve it.

Mrs. Ford. Nay, I must tell you, so you do,
or else I could not be in that mind.

Rob. [*Within.*] Mistress Ford! Mistress Ford! 92
here's Mistress Page at the door, sweating and
blowing and looking wildly, and would needs
speak with you presently.

Fal. She shall not see me: I will ensconce 96
me behind the arras.

Mrs. Ford. Pray you, do so: she's a very
tattling woman.   [*Falstaff hides himself.*]

[*Enter Mistress Page and Robin.*]

What's the matter? how now!   100

Mrs. Page. O Mistress Ford! what have you
done? You're shamed, you are overthrown,
you're undone for ever!

Mrs. Ford. What's the matter, good Mistress 104
Page?

Mrs. Page. O well-a-day, Mistress Ford! having an honest man to your husband, to give him
such cause of suspicion!   108

Mrs. Ford. What cause of suspicion?

Mrs. Page. What cause of suspicion! Out
upon you! how am I mistook in you!

Mrs. Ford. Why, alas, what's the matter?   112

85 Counter-gate: *gate of debtors' prison*   96 ensconce: *concea.*
97 arras: *hanging screen of tapestry placed round the walls of a
room*

Mrs. Page. Your husband's coming hither, woman, with all the officers in Windsor, to search for a gentleman that he says is here now in the house by your consent, to take an ill advantage 116 of his absence: you are undone.

Mrs. Ford. [*Aside.*] Speak louder.—'Tis not so, I hope.

Mrs. Page. Pray heaven it be not so, that you 120 have such a man here! but 'tis most certain your husband's coming with half Windsor at his heels, to search for such a one. I come before to tell you. If you know yourself clear, why, I am 124 glad of it; but if you have a friend here, convey, convey him out. Be not amazed; call all your senses to you: defend your reputation, or bid farewell to your good life for ever.   128

Mrs. Ford. What shall I do?—There is a gentleman, my dear friend; and I fear not mine own shame so much as his peril: I had rather than a thousand pound he were out of the house.   132

Mrs. Page. For shame! never stand 'you had rather' and 'you had rather': your husband's here at hand; bethink you of some conveyance: in the house you cannot hide him. 136 O, how have you deceived me! Look, here is a basket: if he be of any reasonable stature, he may creep in here; and throw foul linen upon him, as if it were going to bucking: or—it is 140 whiting-time—send him by your two men to Datchet-mead.

Mrs. Ford. He's too big to go in there. What shall I do?   144

Fal. [*Coming forward.*] Let me see 't, let me

---

124 clear: *innocent*   133 stand: *lose time over*
140 bucking: *washing*   141 whiting-time: *bleaching-time*

see 't, O, let me see 't! I'll in, I'll in. Follow
your friend's counsel. I'll in.

Mrs. Page. What, Sir John Falstaff! Are 148
these your letters, knight?

Fal. I love thee, and none but thee; help me
away: let me creep in here. I'll never—

> [*Gets into the basket; they cover*
> *him with foul linen.*]

Mrs. Page. Help to cover your master, boy. 152
Call your men, Mistress Ford. You dissembling
knight!

Mrs. Ford. What, John! Robert! John!   155
> [*Exit Robin.*]

[*Enter Servants.*]

Go take up these clothes here quickly; where's the
cowl-staff? look, how you drumble! carry them
to the laundress in Datchet-mead; quickly, come.

[*Enter Ford, Page, Caius, and Sir Hugh Evans.*]

Ford. Pray you, come near: if I suspect
without cause, why then make sport at me; 160
then let me be your jest; I deserve it. How
now! what goes here? whither bear you this?

Serv. To the laundress, forsooth.

Mrs. Ford. Why, what have you to do whither 164
they bear it? You were best meddle with buck-
washing.

Ford. Buck! I would I could wash myself of
the buck! Buck, buck, buck! Ay, buck; I war- 168
rant you, buck; and of the season too; it shall
appear.   [*Exeunt Servants with the basket.*]
Gentlemen, I have dreamed to-night; I'll tell

157 cowl-staff: *pole for carrying a basket between two persons*
    drumble: *dawdle*   165 buck-washing: *washing of clothes*
169 of the season: *in season*   171 to-night: *last night*

you my dream. Here, here, here be my keys: 172
ascend my chambers; search, seek, find out: I'll
warrant we'll unkennel the fox. Let me stop this
way first. [*Locking the door.*] So, now uncape.

Page. Good Master Ford, be contented: you 176
wrong yourself too much.

Ford. True, Master Page. Up, gentlemen;
you shall see sport anon: follow me, gentlemen.
[*Exit.*]

Eva. This is fery fantastical humours and 180
jealousies.

Caius. By gar, 'tis no de fashion of France;
it is not jealous in France.

Page. Nay, follow him, gentlemen; see the 184
issue of his search.

[*Exeunt Page, Caius, and Evans.*]

Mrs. Page. Is there not a double excellency
in this?

Mrs. Ford. I know not which pleases me 188
better; that my husband is deceived, or Sir John.

Mrs. Page. What a taking was he in when
your husband asked who was in the basket!

Mrs. Ford. I am half afraid he will have need 192
of washing; so throwing him into the water will
do him a benefit.

Mrs. Page. Hang him, dishonest rascal! I
would all of the same strain were in the same 196
distress.

Mrs. Ford. I think my husband hath some
special suspicion of Falstaff's being here; for I
never saw him so gross in his jealousy till now. 200

Mrs. Page. I will lay a plot to try that; and

174 unkennel: *drive from cover*   175 uncape: *uncouple; cf. n.*
190 taking: *fright*

we will yet have more tricks with Falstaff: his
dissolute disease will scarce obey this medicine.

Mrs. Ford. Shall we send that foolish carrion 204
Mistress Quickly to him, and excuse his throwing into the water; and give him another hope,
to betray him to another punishment?

Mrs. Page. We will do it: let him be sent for 208
to-morrow, eight o'clock, to have amends.

[*Enter Ford, Page, Caius, and Sir Hugh Evans.*]

Ford. I cannot find him: may be the knave
bragged of that he could not compass.

Mrs. Page. [*Aside to Mrs. Ford.*] Heard you 212
that?

Mrs. Ford. [*Aside to Mrs. Page.*] Ay, ay,
peace.—You use me well, Master Ford, do you?

Ford. Ay, I do so.   216

Mrs. Ford. Heaven make you better than
your thoughts!

Ford. Amen!

Mrs. Page. You do yourself mighty wrong, 220
Master Ford.

Ford. Ay, ay; I must bear it.

Eva. If there pe any pody in the house, and
in the chambers, and in the coffers, and in the 224
presses, heaven forgive my sins at the day of
judgment!

Caius. By gar, nor I too, dere is no bodies.

Page. Fie, fie, Master Ford! are you not 228
ashamed? What spirit, what devil suggests this
imagination? I would not ha' your distemper
in this kind for the wealth of Windsor Castle.   231

Ford. 'Tis my fault, Master Page: I suffer for it.

Eva. You suffer for a pad conscience: your

225 presses: *clothespresses*   231 kind: *way*

wife is as honest a 'omans as I will desires among
five thousand, and five hundred too.

Caius. By gar, I see 'tis an honest woman. 236

Ford. Well; I promised you a dinner. Come,
come, walk in the Park: I pray you, pardon me;
I will hereafter make known to you why I have
done this. Come, wife; come, Mistress Page. I 240
pray you, pardon me; pray heartily, pardon me.

Page. Let's go in, gentlemen; but, trust me,
we'll mock him. I do invite you to-morrow
morning to my house to breakfast; after, we'll 244
a-birding together: I have a fine hawk for the
bush. Shall it be so?

Ford. Anything.

Eva. If there is one, I shall make two in the 248
company.

Caius. If dere be one or two, I shall make-a
de turd.

Ford. Pray you go, Master Page.   252

Eva. I pray you now, remembrance to-
morrow on the lousy knave, mine host.

Caius. Dat is good; by gar, vit all my heart.

Eva. A lousy knave! to have his gibes and 256
his mockeries!   *Exeunt.*

Scene Four

[*A Room in Page's House*]

Enter Fenton [*and*] *Anne Page;* [*and later*] *Shallow, Slender,* [*Mistress*] *Quickly, Page,* [*and*]
Mist[*ress*] *Page.*

Fent. I see I cannot get thy father's love;
Therefore no more turn me to him, sweet Nan.

245 a-birding: *hawking; cf. n.*   ? turn: *refer*

Anne. Alas! how then?

Fent. Why, thou must be thyself.
He doth object, I am too great of birth, 4
And that my state being gall'd with my expense,
I seek to heal it only by his wealth.
Besides these, other bars he lays before me,
My riots past, my wild societies; 8
And tells me 'tis a thing impossible
I should love thee but as a property.

Anne. May be he tells you true.

Fent. No, heaven so speed me in my time to
come! 12
Albeit I will confess thy father's wealth
Was the first motive that I woo'd thee, Anne:
Yet, wooing thee, I found thee of more value
Than stamps in gold or sums in sealed bags; 16
And 'tis the very riches of thyself
That now I aim at.

Anne. Gentle Master Fenton,
Yet seek my father's love; still seek it, sir:
If opportunity and humblest suit 20
Cannot attain it, why, then,—hark you hither.

[*They converse apart.*]

[*Enter Shallow, Slender, and Mistress Quickly.*]

Shal. Break their talk, Mistress Quickly: my
kinsman shall speak for himself.

Slen. I'll make a shaft or a bolt on 't. 'Slid, 24
'tis but venturing.

Shal. Be not dismayed.

Slen. No, she shall not dismay me: I care
not for that, but that I am afeard. 28

---

5 state: *estate*   gall'd with my expense: *exhausted by my*
   squandering   16 stamps: *coins*   22 Break: *interrupt*
24 shaft . . . bolt; *cf. n.*   'Slid: *God's eyelid*

Quick. Hark ye; Master Slender would speak
a word with you.

Anne. I come to him. [*Aside.*] This is my
father's choice.

O, what a world of vile ill-favour'd faults   32
Looks handsome in three hundred pounds a year!

Quick. And how does good Master Fenton?
Pray you, a word with you.

Shal. She's coming; to her, coz. O boy, 36
thou hadst a father!

Slen. I had a father, Mistress Anne; my
uncle can tell you good jests of him. Pray you,
uncle, tell Mistress Anne the jest, how my father 40
stole two geese out of a pen, good uncle.

Shal. Mistress Anne, my cousin loves you.

Slen. Ay, that I do; as well as I love any
woman in Gloucestershire.   44

Shal. He will maintain you like a gentlewoman.

Slen. Ay, that I will, come cut and long-tail,
under the degree of a squire.   48

Shal. He will make you a hundred and fifty
pounds jointure.

Anne. Good Master Shallow, let him woo for
himself.   52

Shal. Marry, I thank you for it; I thank you
for that good comfort. She calls you, coz: I'll
leave you.

Anne. Now, Master Slender.   56

Slen. Now, good Mistress Anne.—

Anne. What is your will?

Slen. My will? od's heartlings! that's a pretty
jest, indeed! I ne'er made my will yet, I thank 60

47 cut: *with docked tail*   59 od's heartlings: *God's little heart*

heaven; I am not such a sickly creature, I give
heaven praise.

Anne. I mean, Master Slender, what would
you with me ?   64

Slen. Truly, for mine own part, I would little
or nothing with you. Your father and my
uncle have made motions: if it be my luck, so;
if not, happy man be his dole! They can tell 68
you how things go better than I can: you may
ask your father; here he comes.

[*Enter Page and Mistress Page.*]

Page. Now, Master Slender: love him, daughter
Anne.
Why, how now! what does Master Fenton here?   72
You wrong me, sir, thus still to haunt my house:
I told you, sir, my daughter is dispos'd of.

Fent. Nay, Master Page, be not impatient.

Mrs. Page. Good Master Fenton, come not to my
child.   76

Page. She is no match for you.

Fent. Sir, will you hear me?

Page.   No, good Master Fenton.
Come, Master Shallow; come, son Slender, in.
Knowing my mind, you wrong me, Master Fenton.   80
[*Exeunt Page, Shallow, and Slender.*]

Quick. Speak to Mistress Page.

Fent. Good Mistress Page, for that I love your
daughter
In such a righteous fashion as I do,
Perforce, against all checks, rebukes and manners, 84
I must advance the colours of my love
And not retire: let me have your good will.

68 happy man be his dole: *happiness be his portion (a proverbial
phrase)*   84 checks: *reproofs*   85 colours: *standards*

Anne. Good mother, do not marry me to yond fool.

Mrs. Page. I mean it not; I seek you a better hus-
band.										88

Quick. That's my master, Master Doctor.

Anne. Alas! I had rather be set quick i' the earth,
And bowl'd to death with turnips.

Mrs. Page. Come, trouble not yourself.		Good
	Master Fenton,								92
I will not be your friend nor enemy:
My daughter will I question how she loves you,
And as I find her, so am I affected.
Till then, farewell, sir: she must needs go in;		96
Her father will be angry.

Fent. Farewell, gentle mistress. Farewell, Nan.

							[*Exeunt Mistress Page and Anne.*]

Quick. This is my doing now: 'Nay,' said I,
'will you cast away your child on a fool, and a 100
physician?	Look on Master Fenton.'	This is
my doing.

Fent. I thank thee: and I pray thee, once to-night
Give my sweet Nan this ring. There's for thy
	pains.										104

Quick. Now heaven send thee good fortune!
[*Exit Fenton.*] A kind heart he hath: a woman
would run through fire and water for such a
kind heart.	But yet I would my master had 106
Mistress Anne; or I would Master Slender had
her; or, in sooth, I would Master Fenton had
her.	I will do what I can for them all three,
for so I have promised, and I'll be as good as 112
my word; but speciously for Master Fenton.
Well, I must of another errand to Sir John

90 quick: *alive*											95 affected: *inclined*
103 once: *sometime*							113 speciously: *i.e., especially*

Falstaff from my two mistresses: what a beast
am I to slack it!   [*Exit.*] 116

Scene Five

[*A Room in the Garter Inn*]

*Enter Falstaff [and] Bardolph; [and later Mistress]
Quickly, [and] Ford.*

    Fal. Bardolph, I say,—
    Bard. Here, sir.
    Fal. Go fetch me a quart of sack; put a
toast in 't. [*Exit Bardolph.*] Have I lived to be 4
carried in a basket, and to be thrown in the
Thames like a barrow of butcher's offal? Well,
if I be served such another trick, I'll have my
brains ta'en out, and buttered, and give them to 8
a dog for a new year's gift. The rogues slighted
me into the river with as little remorse as they
would have drowned a blind bitch's puppies,
fifteen i' the litter; and you may know by my 12
size that I have a kind of alacrity in sinking: if
the bottom were as deep as hell, I should down.
I had been drowned but that the shore was
shelvy and shallow; a death that I abhor, for 16
the water swells a man, and what a thing should
I have been when I had been swelled! I should
have been a mountain of mummy.

    [*Enter Bardolph with sack.*]

    Bard. Here's Mistress Quickly, sir, to speak 20
with you.
    Fal. Come, let me pour in some sack to the

9 slighted: *tossed carelessly*   19 mummy: *dead flesk*

Thames water, for my belly's as cold as if I had
swallowed snowballs for pills to cool the reins. 24
Call her in.

Bard. Come in, woman.

[*Enter Mistress Quickly.*]

Quick. By your leave. I cry you mercy: give
your worship good morrow.   28

Fal. Take away these chalices. Go brew me
a pottle of sack finely.

Bard. With eggs, sir?

Fal. Simple of itself; I'll no pullet-sperm in 32
my brewage. [*Exit Bardolph.*]—How now!

Quick. Marry, sir, I come to your worship
from Mistress Ford.

Fal. Mistress Ford! I have had ford enough; 36
I was thrown into the ford; I have my belly full
of ford.

Quick. Alas the day! good heart, that was
not her fault: she does so take on with her 40
men; they mistook their erection.

Fal. So did I mine, to build upon a foolish
woman's promise.

Quick. Well, she laments, sir, for it, that it 44
would yearn your heart to see it. Her husband
goes this morning a-birding: she desires you
once more to come to her between eight and
nine. I must carry her word quickly: she'll 48
make you amends, I warrant you.

Fal. Well, I will visit her: tell her so; and
bid her think what a man is: let her consider
his frailty, and then judge of my merit.   52

24 reins: *kidneys*   27 cry you mercy: *beg your pardon*
30 pottle: *two-quart measure*   41 erection: *i.e., direction*
45 yearn: *grieve*

Quick. I will tell her.

Fal. Do so. Between nine and ten, sayest thou?

Quick. Eight and nine, sir.

Fal. Well, be gone: I will not miss her.   56

Quick. Peace be with you, sir.   [*Exit.*]

Fal. I marvel I hear not of Master Brook; he sent me word to stay within. I like his money well. O! here he comes.   60

[*Enter Ford.*]

Ford. Bless you, sir!

Fal. Now, Master Brook, you come to know what hath passed between me and Ford's wife?   64

Ford. That, indeed, Sir John, is my business.

Fal. Master Brook, I will not lie to you: I was at her house the hour she appointed me.   68

Ford. And sped you, sir?

Fal. Very ill-favouredly, Master Brook.

Ford. How so, sir? did she change her determination?   72

Fal. No, Master Brook; but the peaking cornuto her husband, Master Brook, dwelling in a continual 'larum of jealousy, comes me in the instant of our encounter, after we had embraced, 76 kissed, protested, and, as it were, spoke the prologue of our comedy; and at his heels a rabble of his companions, thither provoked and instigated by his distemper, and, forsooth, to 80 search his house for his wife's love.

Ford. What! while you were there?

70 ill-favouredly: *badly*   73 peaking: *sneaking*
74 cornuto: *cuckold*   75 'larum: *alarm*
80 distemper: *ill humour*

Fal. While I was there.

Ford. And did he search for you, and could 84
not find you?

Fal. You shall hear. As good luck would
have it, comes in one Mistress Page; gives intelligence of Ford's approach; and in her 88
invention, and Ford's wife's distraction, they
conveyed me into a buck-basket.

Ford. A buck-basket!

Fal. By the Lord, a buck-basket! rammed 92
me in with foul shirts and smocks, socks, foul
stockings, greasy napkins; that, Master Brook,
there was the rankest compound of villainous
smell that ever offended nostril.   96

Ford. And how long lay you there?

Fal. Nay, you shall hear, Master Brook, what
I have suffered to bring this woman to evil for
your good. Being thus crammed in the basket, 100
a couple of Ford's knaves, his hinds, were called
forth by their mistress to carry me in the name
of foul clothes to Datchet-lane: they took me
on their shoulders; met the jealous knave their 104
master in the door, who asked them once or
twice what they had in their basket. I quaked
for fear lest the lunatic knave would have
searched it; but Fate, ordaining he should be a 108
cuckold, held his hand. Well; on went he for a
search, and away went I for foul clothes. But
mark the sequel, Master Brook: I suffered the
pangs of three several deaths: first, an intoler- 112
able fright, to be detected with a jealous rotten
bell-wether; next, to be compassed, like a good

94 that: *so that*   101 hinds: *servants*   113 with: *by*

bilbo, in the circumference of a peck, hilt to
point, heel to head; and then, to be stopped in, 116
like a strong distillation, with stinking clothes
that fretted in their own grease: think of that,
a man of my kidney, think of that, that am as
subject to heat as butter; a man of continual 120
dissolution and thaw: it was a miracle to 'scape
suffocation.   And in the height of this bath,
when I was more than half stewed in grease,
like a Dutch dish, to be thrown into the Thames, 124
and cooled, glowing hot, in that surge, like a
horse-shoe; think of that, hissing hot, think of
that, Master Brook!

Ford. In good sadness, sir, I am sorry that for 128
my sake you have suffered all this.   My suit then
is desperate; you'll undertake her no more?

Fal. Master Brook, I will be thrown into
Etna, as I have been into Thames, ere I will 132
leave her thus.   Her husband is this morning
gone a-birding: I have received from her another
embassy of meeting; 'twixt eight and nine is
the hour, Master Brook.   136

Ford. 'Tis past eight already, sir.

Fal. Is it? I will then address me to my appointment.   Come to me at your convenient
leisure, and you shall know how I speed, and 140
the conclusion shall be crowned with your en-
joying her: adieu.   You shall have her, Master
Brook; Master Brook, you shall cuckold Ford.

                                              [*Exit.*]

Ford. Hum! ha! is this a vision? is this a 144
dream? do I sleep? Master Ford, awake! awake,

115 bilbo; *cf. n.*   118 fretted: *consumed*
128 sadness: *seriousness*   135 embassy: *message*
138 address: *prepare*

Master Ford! there's a hole made in your best
coat, Master Ford. This 'tis to be married: this
'tis to have linen and buck-baskets! Well, I 148
will proclaim myself what I am: I will now take
the lecher; he is at my house; he cannot 'scape
me; 'tis impossible he should; he cannot creep
into a half-penny purse, nor into a pepper-box; 152
but, lest the devil that guides him should aid
him, I will search impossible places. Though
what I am I cannot avoid, yet to be what I would
not, shall not make be tame: if I have horns to 156
make one mad, let the proverb go with me; I'll be
horn-mad.   [*Exit.*]

ACT FOURTH

Scene One

[A Street]

Enter Mistress Page, [Mistress] Quickly, [and] Wil-
liam; [and later] Evans.

Mrs. Page. Is he at Master Ford's already,
thinkest thou?

Quick. Sure he is by this, or will be presently;
but truly, he is very courageous mad about his 4
throwing into the water. Mistress Ford desires
you to come suddenly.

Mrs. Page. I'll be with her by and by: I'll
but bring my young man here to school. Look, 8
where his master comes; 'tis a playing-day,
I see.

[Enter Sir Hugh Evans.]

6 suddenly: *at once*   7 by and by: *immediately*

How now, Sir Hugh! no school to-day?

Eva. No; Master Slender is let the boys 12
leave to play.

Quick. Blessing of his heart!

Mrs. Page. Sir Hugh, my husband says my
son profits nothing in the world at his book: I 16
pray you, ask him some questions in his acci-
dence.

Eva. Come hither, William; hold up your
head; come.   20

Mrs. Page. Come on, sirrah; hold up your
head; answer your master, be not afraid.

Eva. William, how many numbers is in nouns?

Will. Two.   24

Quick. Truly, I thought there had been one
number more, because they say, 'Od's nouns.'

Eva. Peace your tattlings! What is *fair*,
William?   28

Will. *Pulcher.*

Quick. Polecats! there are fairer things than
polecats, sure.

Eva. You are a very simplicity 'oman: I pray 32
you peace. What is *lapis*, William?

Will. A stone.

Eva. And what is *a stone*, William?

Will. A pebble.   36

Eva. No, it is *lapis:* I pray you remember in
your prain.

Will. *Lapis.*

Eva. That is a good William. What is he, 40
William, that does lend articles?

Will. Articles are borrowed of the pronoun,

26 Od's nouns: *God's wounds*

and be thus declined, *Singulariter, nominativo, hic, hæc, hoc.*   44

Eva. *Nominativo, hig, hag, hog*; pray you, mark: *genitivo, hujus.* Well, what is your accusative case?

Will. *Accusativo, hinc.*   48

Eva. I pray you, have your remembrance, child; *accusativo, hung, hang, hog.*

Quick. Hang-hog is Latin for bacon, I warrant you.   52

Eva. Leave your prabbles, 'oman. What is the focative case, William?

Will. O *vocativo, O.*

Eva. Remember, William; focative is *caret.* 56

Quick. And that's a good root.

Eva. 'Oman, forbear.

Mrs. Page. Peace!

Eva. What is your genitive case plural, 60 William?

Will. Genitive case?

Eva. Ay.

Will. *Genitive, horum, harum, horum.*   64

Quick. Vengeance of Jenny's case! fie on her! Never name her, child, if she be a whore.

Eva. For shame, 'oman!

Quick. You do ill to teach the child such 68 words. He teaches him to hick and to hack, which they'll do fast enough of themselves, and to call 'horum'; fie upon you!

Eva. 'Oman, art thou lunatics? hast thou no 72 understandings for thy cases and the numbers of the genders? Thou art as foolish Christian creatures as I would desires.

51 Hang-hog; *cf. n.*
56 caret: *is wanting* (*Latin*)
69 hick: *hiccup*

Mrs. Page. Prithee, hold thy peace.   76

Eva. Show me now, William, some declensions of your pronouns.

Will. Forsooth, I have forgot.

Eva. It is *qui, quæ, quod;* if you forget your 80
quis, your *quæs,* and your *quods,* you must be preeches. Go your ways and play; go.

Mrs. Page. He is a better scholar than I thought he was.   84

Eva. He is a good sprag memory. Farewell, Mistress Page.

Mrs. Page. Adieu, good Sir Hugh. [*Exit Sir Hugh.*] Get you home, boy. Come, we stay too 88 long.   *Exeunt.*

Scene Two

[*A Room in Ford's House*]

Enter Falstaff, Mist[ress] Ford; [and later] Mist[ress] Page, Servants, Ford, Page, Caius, Evans, [and] Shallow.

Fal. Mistress Ford, your sorrow hath eaten up my sufferance. I see you are obsequious in your love, and I profess requital to a hair's breadth; not only, Mistress Ford, in the simple 4 office of love, but in all the accoutrement, complement and ceremony of it. But are you sure of your husband now?

Mrs. Ford. He's a-birding, sweet Sir John. 8

Mrs. Page. [*Within.*] What ho! gossip Ford! what ho!

82 preeches: *i.e., breeched, flogged*   85 sprag: *i.e., sprack, alert*
2 sufferance: *sufferings*   obsequious: *devoted*
9 gossip: *friend*

Mrs. Ford. Step into the chamber, Sir John.
[*Exit Falstaff.*]

[*Enter Mistress Page.*]

Mrs. Page. How now, sweetheart! who's at 12
home besides yourself?

Mrs. Ford. Why, none but mine own people.

Mrs. Page. Indeed!

Mrs. Ford. No, certainly.—[*Aside to her.*] 16
Speak louder.

Mrs. Page. Truly, I am so glad you have nobody here.

Mrs. Ford. Why?   20

Mrs. Page. Why, woman, your husband is in
his old lines again: he so takes on yonder with
my husband; so rails against all married man-
kind; so curses all Eve's daughters, of what com- 24
plexion soever; and so buffets himself on the
forehead, crying, 'Peer out, peer out!' that any
madness I ever yet beheld seemed but tameness,
civility and patience, to this his distemper he 28
is in now. I am glad the fat knight is not
here.

Mrs. Ford. Why, does he talk of him?

Mrs. Page. Of none but him; and swears he 32
was carried out, the last time he searched for
him, in a basket: protests to my husband he is
now here, and hath drawn him and the rest of
their company from their sport, to make another 36
experiment of his suspicion. But I am glad the
knight is not here; now he shall see his own
foolery.

Mrs. Ford. How near is he, Mistress Page? 40

Mrs. Page. Hard by; at street end; he will
be here anon.

Mrs. Ford. I am undone! the knight is here.

Mrs. Page. Why then you are utterly shamed, 44
and he's but a dead man. What a woman are
you! Away with him, away with him! better
shame than murder.

Mrs. Ford. Which way should he go? how 48
should I bestow him? Shall I put him into the
basket again?

[*Enter Falstaff.*]

Fal. No, I'll come no more i' the basket.
May I not go out ere he come?   **52**

Mrs. Page. Alas! three of Master Ford's broth-
ers watch the door with pistols, that none
shall issue out; otherwise you might slip away
ere he came. But what make you here?   **56**

Fal. What shall I do? I'll creep up into the
chimney.

Mrs. Ford. There they always use to discharge their birding-pieces.   **60**

Mrs. Page. Creep into the kiln-hole.

Fal. Where is it?

Mrs. Ford. He will seek there, on my word.
Neither press, coffer, chest, trunk, well, vault, 64
but he hath an abstract for the remembrance of
such places, and goes to them by his note: there
is no hiding you in the house.

Fal. I'll go out, then.   **68**

Mrs. Page. If you go out in your own semblance, you die, Sir John. Unless you go out
disguised,—

---

59 use: *are accustomed*   65 abstract: *catalogue*

Mrs. Ford. How might we disguise him?   72

Mrs. Page. Alas the day! I know not. There
is no woman's gown big enough for him; otherwise, he might put on a hat, a muffler, and a
kerchief, and so escape.   76

Fal. Good hearts, devise something: any extremity rather than a mischief.

Mrs. Ford. My maid's aunt, the fat woman of
Brainford, has a gown above.   80

Mrs. Page. On my word, it will serve him;
she's as big as he is: and there's her thrummed
hat and her muffler too. Run up, Sir John.

Mrs. Ford. Go, go, sweet Sir John: Mistress 84
Page and I will look some linen for your head.

Mrs. Page. Quick, quick! we'll come dress
you straight; put on the gown the while.

                              [*Exit Falstaff.*]

Mrs. Ford. I would my husband would meet 88
him in this shape: he cannot abide the old woman
of Brainford; he swears she's a witch; forbade
her my house, and hath threatened to beat her.

Mrs. Page. Heaven guide him to thy hus- 92
band's cudgel, and the devil guide his cudgel
afterwards!

Mrs. Ford. But is my husband coming?

Mrs. Page. Ay, in good sadness, is he; and 96
talks of the basket too, howsoever he hath had
intelligence.

Mrs. Ford. We'll try that; for I'll appoint
my men to carry the basket again, to meet him 100
at the door with it, as they did last time.

Mrs. Page. Nay, but he'll be here presently:
let's go dress him like the witch of Brainford.

79, 80 fat woman of Brainford; *cf. n.*
82 thrummed: *made of coarse yarn*

Mrs. Ford. I'll first direct my men what they 104
shall do with the basket. Go up; I'll bring
linen for him straight.   [*Exit.*]

Mrs. Page. Hang him, dishonest varlet! we
cannot misuse him enough.   108
We'll leave a proof, by that which we will **do**,
Wives may be merry, and yet honest too:
We do not act that often jest and laugh;
'Tis old but true, 'Still swine eats all the draff.' 112
          [*Exit.*]

[*Enter Mistress Ford, and two servants.*]

Mrs. Ford. Go, sirs, take the basket again on
your shoulders: your master is hard at door; if
he bid you set it down, obey him. Quickly;
dispatch.   [*Exit.*] 116

First Serv. Come, come, take it up.

Sec. Serv. Pray heaven, it be not full of knight
again.

First Serv. I hope not; I had as lief bear so 120
much lead.

[*Enter Ford, Page, Shallow, Caius, and Sir Hugh
Evans.*]

Ford. Ay, but if it prove true, Master Page,
have you any way then to unfool me again? Set
down the basket, villains. Somebody call my 124
wife. Youth in a basket! O you panderly rascals! there's a knot, a ging, a pack, a conspiracy
against me: now shall the devil be shamed.
What, wife, I say! Come, come forth! Be- 128
hold what honest clothes you send forth to
bleaching!

107 dishonest: *unchaste*   112 draff: *swill*
116 dispatch: *hasten*   126 ging: *gang*   pack: *confederacy*

Page. Why, this passes! Master Ford, you are not to go loose any longer; you must be 132 pinioned.

Eva. Why, this is lunatics! this is mad as a mad dog!

Shal. Indeed, Master Ford, this is not well, 136 indeed.

Ford. So say I too, sir.—

[*Enter Mistress Ford.*]

Come hither Mistress Ford; the honest woman, the modest wife, the virtuous creature, that hath 140 the jealous fool to her husband! I suspect without cause, mistress, do I?

Mrs. Ford. Heaven be my witness, you do, if you suspect me in any dishonesty.   144

Ford. Well said, brazen-face! hold it out. Come forth, sirrah!

[*Pulling clothes out of the basket.*]

Page. This passes!

Mrs. Ford. Are you not ashamed? let the 148 clothes alone.

Ford. I shall find you anon.

Eva. 'Tis unreasonable. Will you take up your wife's clothes? Come away.   152

Ford. Empty the basket, I say!

Mrs. Ford. Why, man, why?

Ford. Master Page, as I am an honest man, there was one conveyed out of my house yester- 156 day in this basket: why may not he be there again? In my house I am sure he is; my intelligence is true; my jealousy is reasonable. Pluck me out all the linen.   160

Mrs. Ford. If you find a man there he shall die a flea's death.

Page. Here's no man.

Shal. By my fidelity, this is not well, Master **164**
Ford, this wrongs you.

Eva. Master Ford, you must pray, and not
follow the imaginations of your own heart: this
is jealousies.   **168**

Ford. Well, he's not here I seek for.

Page. No, nor nowhere else but in your brain.

Ford. Help to search my house this one time:
if I find not what I seek, show no colour for my **172**
extremity; let me for ever be your table-sport;
let them say of me, 'As jealous as Ford, that
searched a hollow walnut for his wife's leman.'
Satisfy me once more; once more search with **176**
me.

Mrs. Ford. What ho, Mistress Page! come
you and the old woman down; my husband will
come into the chamber.   **180**

Ford. Old woman! What old woman's that?

Mrs. Ford. Why, it is my maid's aunt of
Brainford.

Ford. A witch, a quean, an old cozening **184**
quean! Have I not forbid her my house? She
comes of errands, does she? We are simple
men; we do not know what's brought to pass
under the profession of fortune-telling. She **188**
works by charms, by spells, by the figure, and
such daubery as this is, beyond our element: we
know nothing. Come down, you witch, you hag,
you; come down, I say!   **192**

Mrs. Ford. Nay, good, sweet husband! good
gentlemen, let him not strike the old woman.

---

172 show no colour: *suggest no excuse*   173 extremity: *extravagance*
175 leman: *lover*   184 quean: *hussy*   cozening: *deceiving*
189 figure: *effigy; cf. n.*   190 daubery: *false show*

[Enter Falstaff in woman's clothes, and Mistress Page.]

Mrs. Page. Come, Mother Prat; come, give me your hand.   196

Ford. I'll 'prat' her.—[*Beating him.*] Out of my door, you witch, you rag, you baggage, you polecat, you ronyon! out, out! I'll conjure you, I'll fortune-tell you.   [*Exit Falstaff.*] 200

Mrs. Page. Are you not ashamed? I think you have killed the poor woman.

Mrs. Ford. Nay, he will do it. 'Tis a goodly credit for you.   204

Ford. Hang her, witch!

Eva. By yea and no, I think the 'oman is a witch indeed: I like not when a 'oman has a great peard; I spy a great peard under his 208 muffler.

Ford. Will you follow, gentlemen? I beseech you, follow: see but the issue of my jealousy. If I cry out thus upon no trail, never trust me 212 when I open again.

Page. Let's obey his humour a little further. Come, gentlemen.

[Exeunt Ford, Page, Shallow, Caius, and Evans.]

Mrs. Page. Trust me, he beat him most 216 pitifully.

Mrs. Ford. Nay, by the mass, that he did not; he beat him most unpitifully methought.

Mrs. Page. I'll have the cudgel hallowed 220 and hung o'er the altar: it hath done meritorious service.

Mrs. Ford. What think you? May we, with the warrant of womanhood and the witness of 224

199 ronyon: *mangy woman*

a good conscience, pursue him with any further
revenge?

Mrs. Page. The spirit of wantonness is, sure,
scared out of him: if the devil have him not in 228
fee-simple, with fine and recovery, he will never,
I think, in the way of waste, attempt us again.

Mrs. Ford. Shall we tell our husbands how
we have served him?   232

Mrs. Page. Yes, by all means; if it be but to
scrape the figures out of your husband's brains.
If they can find in their hearts the poor un-
virtuous fat knight shall be any further afflicted, 236
we two will still be the ministers.

Mrs. Ford. I'll warrant they'll have him
publicly shamed, and methinks there would be
no period to the jest, should he not be publicly 240
shamed.

Mrs. Page. Come, to the forge with it then;
shape it: I would not have things cool.   *Exeunt.*

Scene Three

[*A Room in the Garter Inn*]

Enter Host and Bardolph.

Bard. Sir, the Germans desire to have three
of your horses: the duke himself will be to-morrow at court, and they are going to meet him.

Host. What duke should that be comes so 4
secretly? I hear not of him in the court. Let
me speak with the gentlemen; they speak
English?

229 fee-simple: *absolute possession*   fine and recovery; *cf. n.*
230 waste: *spoliation*   234 figures: *phantasms*
237 ministers: *agents*   240 period: *fitting conclusion*
1 Germans; *cf. n.*

Bard. Ay, sir; I'll call them to you.   8

Host. They shall have my horses, but I'll
make them pay; I'll sauce them: they have
had my house a week at command; I have
turned away my other guests: they must come 12
off; I'll sauce them. Come.   *Exeunt.*

Scene Four

[*A Room in Ford's House*]

*Enter Page, Ford, Mistress Page, Mistress Ford,
and Evans.*

Eva. 'Tis one of the pest discretions of a
'oman as ever I did look upon.

Page. And did he send you both these letters
at an instant?   4

Mrs. Page. Within a quarter of an hour.

Ford. Pardon me, wife. Henceforth do what
thou wilt;

I rather will suspect the sun with cold

Than thee with wantonness: now doth thy honour
stand,   8

In him that was of late an heretic,

As firm as faith.

Page.   'Tis well, 'tis well; no more.

Be not as extreme in submission

As in offence;   12

But let our plot go forward: let our wives

Yet once again, to make us public sport,

Appoint a meeting with this old fat fellow,

Where we may take him and disgrace him for it. 16

12, 13 come off: *pay down*

Ford. There is no better way than that they
spoke of.

Page. How? to send him word they'll meet
him in the Park at midnight? Fie, fie! he'll
never come.   20

Eva. You say he has been thrown into the
rivers, and has been grievously peaten as an old
'oman: methinks there should be terrors in him
that he should not come; methinks his flesh is 24
punished, he shall have no desires.

Page. So think I too.

Mrs. Ford. Devise but how you'll use him when
he comes,
And let us two devise to bring him thither.   28

Mrs. Page. There is an old tale goes that Herne
the hunter,
Sometime a keeper here in Windsor forest,
Doth all the winter-time, at still midnight,
Walk round about an oak, with great ragg'd
horns;   32
And there he blasts the tree, and takes the cattle,
And makes milch-kine yield blood, and shakes a
chain
In a most hideous and dreadful manner:
You have heard of such a spirit, and well you
know   36
The superstitious idle-headed eld
Receiv'd and did deliver to our age
This tale of Herne the hunter for a truth.

Page. Why, yet there want not many that do
fear   40
In deep of night to walk by this Herne's oak.

33 biasts: *blights*   takes: *bewitches*
37 eld: *people of olden time*

But what of this?

    Mrs. Ford.   Marry, this is our device;
That Falstaff at that oak shall meet with us,
[Disguis'd like Herne with huge horns on his
    head.]   44

    Page. Well, let it not be doubted but he'll come,
And in this shape when you have brought him
    thither,
What shall be done with him? what is your plot?

    Mrs. Page. That likewise have we thought upon,
    and thus: 48
Nan Page my daughter, and my little son,
And three or four more of their growth, we'll dress
Like urchins, ouphs, and fairies, green and white,
With rounds of waxen tapers on their heads,   52
And rattles in their hands. Upon a sudden,
As Falstaff, she, and I, are newly met,
Let them from forth a sawpit rush at once
With some diffused song: upon their sight,   56
We two in great amazedness will fly:
Then let them all encircle him about,
And, fairy-like, to-pinch the unclean knight;
And ask him why, that hour of fairy revel,   60
In their so sacred paths he dares to tread
In shape profane.

    Mrs. Ford.   And till he tell the truth,
Let the supposed fairies pinch him sound
And burn him with their tapers.

    Mrs. Page.   The truth being known, 64
We'll all present ourselves, dis-horn the spirit,
And mock him home to Windsor.

    Ford.   The children must
Be practis'd well to this, or they'll ne'er do 't.

51 urchins: *goblins*   ouphs: *elves*   56 diffused: *confused*
59 to-pinch: *pinch soundly*   63 sound: *soundly*

Eva. I will teach the children their be- 68
haviours; and I will be like a jack-an-apes
also, to burn the knight with my taber.

Ford. That will be excellent. I'll go buy
them vizards.   72

Mrs. Page. My Nan shall be the queen of all the
fairies,
Finely attired in a robe of white.

Page. That silk will I go buy:—[*Aside.*] and in
that time
Shall Master Slender steal my Nan away,   76
And marry her at Eton. Go, send to Falstaff
straight.

Ford. Nay, I'll to him again in name of Brook;
He'll tell me all his purpose. Sure, he'll come.

Mrs. Page. Fear not you that. Go, get us prop-
erties,   80
And tricking for our fairies.

Eva. Let us about it: it is admirable pleas-
ures and fery honest knaveries.
                          [*Exeunt Page, Ford, and Evans.*]

Mrs. Page. Go, Mistress Ford,   84
Send Quickly to Sir John, to know his mind.
                                    [*Exit Mistress Ford.*]
I'll to the doctor: he hath my good will,
And none but he, to marry with Nan Page.
That Slender, though well landed, is an idiot;   88
And him my husband best of all affects:
The doctor is well money'd, and his friends
Potent at court: he, none but he, shall have her,
Though twenty thousand worthier come to crave
her.   [*Exit.*] 92

Scene Five

[A Room in the Garter Inn]

Enter Host [and] Simple; [and later] Falstaff, Bardolph, Evans, Caius, [and Mistress] Quickly.

Host. What wouldst thou have, boor? what, thick-skin? speak, breathe, discuss; brief, short, quick, snap.

Sim. Marry, sir, I come to speak with Sir 4 John Falstaff from Master Slender.

Host. There's his chamber, his house, his castle, his standing-bed and truckle-bed: 'tis painted about with the story of the Prodigal, 8 fresh and new. Go knock and call: he'll speak like an Anthropophaginian unto thee: knock, I say.

Sim. There's an old woman, a fat woman, 12 gone up into his chamber: I'll be so bold as stay, sir, till she come down; I come to speak with her, indeed.

Host. Ha! a fat woman! the knight may be 16 robbed: I'll call. Bully knight! Bully Sir John! speak from thy lungs military: art thou there? it is thine host, thine Ephesian, calls.

Fal. [*Above.*] How now, mine host!   20

Host. Here's a Bohemian-Tartar tarries the coming down of thy fat woman. Let her descend, bully; let her descend; my chambers are honourable: fie! privacy? fie!   24

[Enter Falstaff.]

7 truckle-bed: *trundle-bed, pushed under standing-bed when not in use*
10 Anthropophaginian: *cannibal*
19 Ephesian: *boon companion*
21 Bohemian-Tartar: *wild fellow*

Fal. There was, mine host, an old fat woman
even now with me, but she's gone.

Sim. Pray you, sir, was 't not the wise woman
of Brainford?   28

Fal. Ay, marry, was it, mussel-shell: what
would you with her?

Sim. My master, sir, Master Slender, sent to
her, seeing her go thorough the streets, to know, 32
sir, whether one Nym, sir, that beguiled him of
a chain, had the chain or no.

Fal. I spake with the old woman about it.

Sim. And what says she, I pray, sir?   36

Fal. Marry, she says that the very same man
that beguiled Master Slender of his chain
cozened him of it.

Sim. I would I could have spoken with the 40
woman herself: I had other things to have
spoken with her too, from him.

Fal. What are they? let us know.

Host. Ay, come; quick.   44

Sim. I may not conceal them, sir.

Host. Conceal them, or thou diest.

Sim. Why, sir, they were nothing but about
Mistress Anne Page; to know if it were my 48
master's fortune to have her or no.

Fal. 'Tis, 'tis his fortune.

Sim. What, sir?

Fal. To have her, or no. Go; say the 52
woman told me so.

Sim. May I be bold to say so, sir?

Fal. Ay, sir: like who more bold?

Sim. I thank your worship: I shall make my 56
master glad with these tidings.   [*Exit.*]

29 mussel-shell; *cf. n.*   32 thorough: *through*
45 conceal: *i.e., reveal*   55 like . . . bold: *like the boldest*

Host. Thou art clerkly, thou art clerkly, Sir John. Was there a wise woman with thee?

Fal. Ay, that there was, mine host; one that 60 hath taught me more wit than ever I learned before in my life: and I paid nothing for it neither, but was paid for my learning.

[*Enter Bardolph.*]

Bard. Out, alas, sir! cozenage, mere cozenage! 64

Host. Where be my horses? speak well of them, varletto.

Bard. Run away, with the cozeners; for so soon as I came beyond Eton, they threw me off, 68 from behind one of them, in a slough of mire; and set spurs and away, like three German devils, three Doctor Faustuses.

Host. They are gone but to meet the duke, 72 villain. Do not say they be fled: Germans are honest men.

[*Enter Sir Hugh Evans.*]

Eva. Where is mine host?

Host. What is the matter, sir?   76

Eva. Have a care of your entertainments: there is a friend of mine come to town, tells me, there is three cozen-germans that has cozened all the hosts of Readins, of Maidenhead, of 80 Colebrook, of horses and money. I tell you for good will, look you: you are wise and full of gibes and vlouting-stogs, and 'tis not convenient you should be cozened. Fare you well.   [*Exit.*] 84

[*Enter Doctor Caius.*]

58 clerkly: *scholarly*   64 mere: *pure*
66 varletto: *rascal servant*   71 Doctor Faustuses; *cf. n.*
79 cozen-germans; *cf. n.*   80 Readins: *Reading*
81 Colebrook: *Colnbrook, four miles east of Windsor*

Caius. Vere is mine host de Jarteer?

Host. Here, Master Doctor, in perplexity and doubtful dilemma.

Caius. I cannot tell vat is dat; but it is tell-a 88 me dat you make grand preparation for a duke de Jamany: by my trot, dere is no duke dat de court is know to come. I tell you for good vill: adieu.   [*Exit.*] 92

Host. Hue and cry, villain! go. Assist me, knight; I am undone. Fly, run, hue and cry, villain! I am undone!

[*Exeunt Host and Bardolph.*]

Fal. I would all the world might be cozened, 96 for I have been cozened and beaten too. If it should come to the ear of the court how I have been transformed, and how my transformation hath been washed and cudgelled, they would 100 melt me out of my fat drop by drop, and liquor fishermen's boots with me: I warrant they would whip me with their fine wits till I were as crest-fallen as a dried pear. I never pros- 104 pered since I forswore myself at primero. Well, if my mind were but long enough to say my prayers, I would repent.

[*Enter Mistress Quickly.*]

Now, whence come you?   108

Quick. From the two parties, forsooth.

Fal. The devil take one party and his dam the other! and so they shall be both bestowed. I have suffered more for their sakes, more than 112 the villainous inconstancy of man's disposition is able to bear.

90 Jamany: *i.e., Germany*   101 liquor: *grease*
104 crest-fallen . . . pear; *cf. n.*   105 primero: *a card game*

Quick. And have not they suffered? Yes, I
warrant; speciously one of them: Mistress Ford, 116
good heart, is beaten black and blue, that you
cannot see a white spot about her.

Fal. What tellest thou me of black and blue?
I was beaten myself into all the colours of the 120
rainbow; and I was like to be apprehended for
the witch of Brainford: but that my admirable
dexterity of wit, my counterfeiting the action
of an old woman, delivered me, the knave con- 124
stable had set me i' the stocks, i' the common
stocks, for a witch.

Quick. Sir, let me speak with you in your
chamber; you shall hear how things go, and, I 128
warrant, to your content. Here is a letter will
say somewhat. Good hearts! what ado here is
to bring you together! Sure, one of you does
not serve heaven well, that you are so crossed. 132

Fal. Come up into my chamber.   *Exeunt.*

Scene Six

[Another Room in the Garter Inn]

Enter Fenton [and] Host.

Host. Master Fenton, talk not to me: my
mind is heavy; I will give over all.

Fent. Yet hear me speak. Assist me in my purpose,

And, as I am a gentleman, I'll give thee   4
A hundred pound in gold more than your loss.

Host. I will hear you, Master Fenton; and I
will, at the least, keep your counsel.

132 crossed: *thwarted*

Fent. From time to time I have acquainted you   8
With the dear love I bear to fair Anne Page;
Who mutually hath answer'd my affection,
So far forth as herself might be her chooser,
Even to my wish.   I have a letter from her   12
Of such contents as you will wonder at;
The mirth whereof so larded with my matter,
That neither singly can be manifested,
Without the show of both; wherein fat Falstaff   16
Hath a great scene: the image of the jest
I'll show you here at large. [*Showing the letter.*]
     Hark, good mine host:
To-night at Herne's oak, just 'twixt twelve and one,
Must my sweet Nan present the Fairy Queen;   20
The purpose why, is here: in which disguise,
While other jests are something rank on foot,
Her father hath commanded her to slip
Away with Slender, and with him at Eton   24
Immediately to marry: she hath consented:
Now, sir,
Her mother, even strong against that match
And firm for Doctor Caius, hath appointed   28
That he shall likewise shuffle her away,
While other sports are tasking of their minds;
And at the deanery, where a priest attends,
Straight marry her: to this her mother's plot   32
She, seemingly obedient, likewise hath
Made promise to the doctor. Now, thus it rests:
Her father means she shall be all in white,
And in that habit, when Slender sees his time   36
To take her by the hand and bid her go,

10 mutually: *reciprocally*   14 larded: *interspersed*
17 image: *idea*   20 present: *represent*
22 something: *somewhat*   rank: *abundantly*
27 even: *equally*   30 tasking: *occupying*

She shall go with him: her mother hath intended,
The better to denote her to the doctor,—
For they must all be mask'd and vizarded— 40
That quaint in green she shall be loose enrob'd,
With ribands pendent, flaring 'bout her head;
And when the doctor spies his vantage ripe,
To pinch her by the hand; and on that token 44
The maid hath given consent to go with him.

Host. Which means she to deceive, father or
mother?

Fent. Both, my good host, to go along with me: 48
And here it rests, that you'll procure the vicar
To stay for me at church 'twixt twelve and one,
And, in the lawful name of marrying,
To give our hearts united ceremony. 52

Host. Well, husband your device; I'll to the
vicar.
Bring you the maid, you shall not lack a priest.

Fent. So shall I evermore be bound to thee;
Besides, I'll make a present recompense. *Exeunt.*

ACT FIFTH

Scene One

[*A Room in the Garter Inn*]

Enter Falstaff [*and Mistress*] *Quickly; and* [*later*]
Ford.

Fal. Prithee, no more prattling; go: I'll
hold. This is the third time; I hope good luck

41 quaint: *elegantly*
52 united ceremony: *union of the marriage rite*
2 hold: *keep the engagement*

lies in odd numbers. Away! go. They say there
is divinity in odd numbers, either in nativity, 4
chance or death. Away!

Quick. I'll provide you a chain, and I'll do
what I can to get you a pair of horns.

Fal. Away, I say; time wears: hold up your 8
head, and mince.   [*Exit Mistress Quickly.*]

[*Enter Ford.*]

How now, Master Brook! Master Brook, the
matter will be known to-night, or never. Be you
in the Park about midnight, at Herne's oak, and 12
you shall see wonders.

Ford. Went you not to her yesterday, sir, as
you told me you had appointed?

Fal. I went to her, Master Brook, as you see, 16
like a poor old man; but I came from her,
Master Brook, like a poor old woman. That
same knave Ford, her husband, hath the finest
mad devil of jealousy in him, Master Brook, that 20
ever governed frenzy. I will tell you: he beat
me grievously, in the shape of a woman; for in
the shape of a man, Master Brook, I fear not
Goliath with a weaver's beam, because I know 24
also life is a shuttle. I am in haste: go along
with me; I'll tell you all, Master Brook. Since
I plucked geese, played truant, and whipped top,
I knew not what it was to be beaten till lately. 28
Follow me: I'll tell you strange things of this
knave Ford, on whom to-night I will be revenged, and I will deliver his wife into your hand.
Follow. Strange things in hand, Master Brook! 32
Follow.   *Exeunt.*

9 mince: *walk prudishly*   **25** life is a shuttle; *cf. n.*

Scene Two

[Windsor Park]

Enter Page, Shallow, [and] Slender.

Page. Come, come; we'll couch i' the castle-
ditch till we see the light of our fairies. Remember, son Slender, my daughter.

Slen. Ay, forsooth; I have spoke with her 4
and we have a nayword how to know one another. I come to her in white, and cry, 'mum';
she cries, 'budget'; and by that we know one
another.   8

Shal. That's good too: but what needs either
your 'mum,' or her 'budget'? the white will
decipher her well enough. It hath struck ten
o'clock.   12

Page. The night is dark; light and spirits
will become it well. Heaven prosper our sport!
No man means evil but the devil, and we shall
know him by his horns. Let's away; follow me. 16
                                                                    Exeunt.

Scene Three

[A Street leading to the Park]

*Enter Mist[ress] Page, Mist[ress] Ford, [and]
Caius.*

Mrs. Page. Master Doctor, my daughter is in
green: when you see your time, take her by the
hand, away with her to the deanery, and dis-

1 couch: *lie*   6, 7 mum . . . budget; *cf. n.*
11 decipher: *indicate*

patch it quickly. Go before into the Park: we **4**
two must go together.

 Caius. I know vat I have to do. Adieu.

 Mrs. Page. Fare you well, sir. [*Exit Caius.*]
My husband will not rejoice so much at the **8**
abuse of Falstaff, as he will chafe at the doctor's
marrying my daughter: but 'tis no matter; better
a little chiding than a great deal of heart-break.

 Mrs. Ford. Where is Nan now and her troop **12**
of fairies, and the Welsh devil, Hugh?

 Mrs. Page. They are all couched in a pit hard
by Herne's oak, with obscured lights; which, at
the very instant of Falstaff's and our meeting, **16**
they will at once display to the night.

 Mrs. Ford. That cannot choose but amaze
him.

 Mrs. Page. If he be not amazed, he will be **20**
mocked; if he be amazed, he will every way be
mocked.

 Mrs. Ford. We'll betray him finely.

 Mrs. Page. Against such lewdsters and their
lechery,   **24**
Those that betray them do no treachery.

 Mrs. Ford. The hour draws on: to the oak,
to the oak!   *Exeunt.*

Scene Four

[*Windsor Park*]

Enter Evans [disguised] and [others as] Fairies.

 Eva. Trib, trib, fairies: come; and remember
your parts: Be pold, I pray you; follow me into

24 lewdsters: *lechers*

the pit, and when I give the watch-'ords, do as I
pid you. Come, come; trib, trib.   *Exeunt.* 4

Scene Five

[Another Part of the Park]

Enter Falstaff [disguised as Herne; and later] Mis-
tress Page, Mistress Ford, Evans, Anne Page,
[and others, as] Fairies; [also] Page, Ford,
[Mistress] Quickly, Slender, Fenton, Caius,
[and] Pistol.

Fal. The Windsor bell hath struck twelve;
the minute draws on. Now, the hot-blooded
gods assist me! Remember, Jove, thou wast a
bull for thy Europa; love set on thy horns. O 4
powerful love! that, in some respects, makes a
beast a man; in some other, a man a beast. You
were also, Jupiter, a swan for the love of Leda;
O omnipotent love! how near the god drew to 8
the complexion of a goose! A fault done first in
the form of a beast; O Jove, a beastly fault!
and then another fault in the semblance of a
fowl: think on 't, Jove; a foul fault! When gods 12
have hot backs, what shall poor men do? For
me, I am here a Windsor stag; and the fattest,
I think, i' the forest: send me a cool rut-time,
Jove, or who can blame me to piss my tallow? 16
Who comes here? my doe?

[Enter Mistress Ford and Mistress Page.]

Mrs. Ford. Sir John! art thou there, my deer?
my male deer?

4 Europa; *cf. n.*   7 Leda; *cf. n.*

Fal. My doe with the black scut! Let the 20
sky rain potatoes; let it thunder to the tune of
'Green Sleeves'; hail kissing-comfits and snow
eringoes; let there come a tempest of provoca-
tion, I will shelter me here. 24

Mrs. Ford. Mistress Page is come with me,
sweetheart.

Fal. Divide me like a brib'd buck, each a
haunch: I will keep my sides to myself, my 28
shoulders for the fellow of this walk, and my
horns I bequeath your husbands. Am I a woodman, ha? Speak I like Herne the hunter?
Why, now is Cupid a child of conscience; he 32
makes restitution. As I am a true spirit, welcome! [*Noise within.*]

Mrs. Page. Alas! what noise?

Mrs. Ford. Heaven forgive our sins! 36

Fal. What should this be?

Mrs. Ford. ⎱
Mrs. Page. ⎰ Away, away! [*They run off.*]

Fal. I think the devil will not have me
damned, lest the oil that is in me should set 40
hell on fire; he would never else cross me
thus.

Enter [*Sir Hugh Evans, disguised as before; Pistol,
as Hobgoblin; Anne Page, and others, as*]
Fairies [*with tapers.*]

Anne. Fairies, black, grey, green, and white,
You moonshine revellers, and shades of night, 44

20 scut: *tail (of a deer)*
21 potatoes: *sweet potatoes (supposed to incite love)*
22 kissing-comfits: *perfumed sweetmeats*
23 eringoes: *candied sea-holly*   27 brib'd: *cut into portions*
29 fellow: *keeper*   walk: *forest*   30 woodman: *hunter; cf. n.*
32 child of conscience; *cf. n.*   42 S.d. Hobgoblin: *Puck*

You orphan heirs of fixed destiny,
Attend your office and your quality.
Crier Hobgoblin, make the fairy oyes.

    Pist. Elves, list your names: silence, you **airy**
      toys!   48
Cricket, to Windsor chimneys shalt thou leap:
Where fires thou find'st unrak'd and hearths un-
    swept,
There pinch the maids as blue as bilberry
Our radiant queen hates sluts and sluttery.   52

    Fal. They are fairies; he that speaks tо thеm
    shall die:
I'll wink and couch: no man their works must eye.
                           [*Lies down upon his face.*]

    Eva. Where's Bede? Go you, and where you find
    a maid
That, ere she sleep, has thrice her prayers said, 56
Raise up the organs of her fantasy,
Sleep she as sound as careless infancy;
But those as sleep and think not on their sins,
Pinch them, arms, legs, backs, shoulders, sides, **and**
    shins.   60

    Anne. About, about!
Search Windsor castle, elves, within and out:
Strew good luck, ouphs, on every sacred room,
That it may stand till the perpetual doom,   64
In state as wholesome as in state 'tis fit,
Worthy the owner, and the owner it.
The several chairs of order look you scour
With juice of balm and every precious flower: 68
Each fair instalment, coat, and several crest,
With loyal blazon, ever more be blest!

45 orphan heirs; *cf. n.*   46 office: *duty*   quality: *profession*
47 oyes: *hear ye!* (*the court crier's call*)   51 bilberry: *blueberry*
54 wink: *close my eyes*   57 *Cf. n.*   67 chairs of order; *cf. n.*
69 instalment: *stall*   70 blazon: *armorial bearings*

And nightly, meadow-fairies, look you sing,
Like to the Garter's compass, in a ring: 72
The expressure that it bears, green let it be,
More fertile-fresh than all the field to see;
And, *Honi soit qui mal y pense* write
In emerald tufts, flowers purple, blue, and white; 76
Like sapphire, pearl, and rich embroidery,
Buckled below fair knighthood's bending knee:
Fairies use flowers for their charactery.
Away! disperse! But, till 'tis one o'clock,   80
Our dance of custom round about the oak
Of Herne the hunter, let us not forget.

    Eva. Pray you, lock hand in hand; yourselves in
      order set;
And twenty glow-worms shall our lanterns be,   84
To guide our measure round about the tree.
But, stay; I smell a man of middle-earth.

    Fal. Heavens defend me from that Welsh
    fairy, lest he transform me to a piece of cheese! 88

    Pist. Vile worm, thou wast o'erlook'd even in thy
    birth.

    Anne. With trial-fire touch me his finger-end:
If he be chaste, the flame will back descend
And turn him to no pain; but if he start,   92
It is the flesh of a corrupted heart.

    Pist. A trial! come.

    Eva.   Come, will this wood take fire?
                 [*They burn him with their tapers.*]

    Fal. Oh, oh, oh!

    Anne. Corrupt, corrupt, and tainted in desire!   96
About him, fairies, sing a scornful rime;
And, as you trip, still pinch him to your time.

---

72 compass: *circle*   73 expressure: *picture*
79 charactery: *writing*   86 middle-earth: *world of mortals*
89 o'erlook'd: *bewitched*

The Song.

'Fie on sinful fantasy!
Fie on lust and luxury!   100
Lust is but a bloody fire,
Kindled with unchaste desire,
Fed in heart, whose flames aspire,
As thoughts do blow them higher and higher.   104
Pinch him, fairies, mutually;
Pinch him for his villainy;
Pinch him, and burn him, and turn him about,
Till candles and star-light and moonshine be out.' 108

[*During this song they pinch Falstaff. Doctor Caius
   comes one way, and steals away a boy in green;
   Slender another way, and takes off a boy in
   white; and Fenton comes, and steals away Anne
   Page. A noise of hunting is heard within. All the
   fairies run away. Falstaff rises.*]

[*Enter Page, Ford, Mistress Page, and Mistress
   Ford.*]

Page. Nay, do not fly: I think we have watch'd you
   now:
Will none but Herne the hunter serve your turn?
   Mrs. Page. I pray you, come, hold up the jest no
   higher.
Now, good Sir John, how like you Windsor wives? 112
See you these, husband? do not these fair yokes
Become the forest better than the town?
   Ford. Now sir, who's a cuckold now? Mas-
ter Brook, Falstaff's a knave, a cuckoldly knave; 116
here are his horns, Master Brook: and, Master

100 luxury: *lasciviousness*   101 bloody fire: *fire in the blood*
105 mutually: *all at once*   113 yokes; *cf. n.*

Brook, he hath enjoyed nothing of Ford's but
his buck-basket, his cudgel, and twenty pounds
of money, which must be paid too, Master Brook; 120
his horses are arrested for it, Master Brook.

Mrs. Ford. Sir John, we have had ill luck;
we could never meet. I will never take you for
my love again, but I will always count you my 124
deer.

Fal. I do begin to perceive that I am made
an ass.

Ford. Ay, and an ox too; both the proofs 128
are extant.

Fal. And these are not fairies? I was three
or four times in the thought they were not
fairies; and yet the guiltiness of my mind, the 132
sudden surprise of my powers, drove the grossness of the foppery into a received belief, in
despite of the teeth of all rime and reason, that
they were fairies. See now how wit may be 136
made a Jack-a-lent, when 'tis upon ill employ-
ment!

Eva. Sir John Falstaff, serve Got, and leave
your desires, and fairies will not pinse you.   140

Ford. Well said, fairy Hugh.

Eva. And leave you your jealousies too, I
pray you.

Ford. I will never mistrust my wife again, 144
till thou art able to woo her in good English.

Fal. Have I laid my brain in the sun and
dried it, that it wants matter to prevent so gross
o'er-reaching as this? Am I ridden with a 148
Welsh goat too? shall I have a coxcomb of

121 arrested: *seized by warrant*   133 powers: *faculties*
134 foppery: *deceit*   149 coxcomb: *fool's cap*

frize? 'Tis time I were choked with a piece of
toasted cheese.

Eva. Seese is not goot to give putter: your 152
pelly is all putter.

Fal. 'Seese' and 'putter'! have I lived to stand
at the taunt of one that makes fritters of English? This is enough to be the decay of lust and 156
late-walking through the realm.

Mrs. Page. Why, Sir John, do you think,
though we would have thrust virtue out of our
hearts by the head and shoulders, and have 160
given ourselves without scruple to hell, that ever
the devil could have made you our delight?

Ford. What, a hodge-pudding? a bag of flax?

Mrs. Page. A puffed man?   164

Page. Old, cold, withered, and of intolerable
entrails?

Ford. And one that is as slanderous as Satan?

Page. And as poor as Job?   168

Ford. And as wicked as his wife?

Eva. And given to fornications, and to taverns,
and sack and wine and metheglins, and to
drinkings and swearings and starings, pribbles 172
and prabbles?

Fal. Well, I am your theme: you have the
start of me; I am dejected; I am not able to
answer the Welsh flannel. Ignorance itself is 176
a plummet o'er me: use me as you will.

Ford. Marry, sir, we'll bring you to Windsor,
to one Master Brook, that you have cozened of
money, to whom you should have been a pander: 180

150 frize: *woollen cloth, made in Wales*
163 hodge-pudding: *pudding of many ingredients* (?)
171 metheglins: *mead, a fermented drink*   175 dejected: *humbled*
176 flannel: *cloth, commonly made in Wales*
176, 177 Ignorance . . . me; *cf. n.*

over and above that you have suffered, I think,
to repay that money will be a biting affliction.
[*Mrs. Ford.* Nay, husband, let that go to make
　amends;

Forgive that sum, and so we'll all be friends.　　184
　Ford. Well, here's my hand: all is forgiven at
　last.]
　Page. Yet be cheerful, knight: thou shalt
eat a posset to-night at my house; where I will
desire thee to laugh at my wife, that now laughs 188
at thee. Tell her, Master Slender hath married
her daughter.
　Mrs. Page. [*Aside.*] Doctors doubt that: if
Anne Page be my daughter, she is, by this, 192
Doctor Caius' wife.

[*Enter Slender.*]

　Slen. Whoa, ho! ho! father Page!
　Page. Son, how now! how now, son! have
you dispatched?　　　　　　　　　　　　　196
　Slen. Dispatched! I'll make the best in
Gloucestershire know on 't; would I were hanged,
la, else!
　Page. Of what, son?　　　　　　　　　　　200
　Slen. I came yonder at Eton to marry Mistress
Anne Page, and she's a great lubberly boy: if it
had not been i' the church, I would have swinged
him, or he should have swinged me. If I did 204
not think it had been Anne Page, would I might
never stir! and 'tis a postmaster's boy.
　Page. Upon my life, then, you took the wrong.
　Slen. What need you tell me that? I think 208
so, when I took a boy for a girl. If I had been

203 swinged: *beaten*　　　　206 postmaster: *master of post horses*

married to him, for all he was in woman's apparel, I would not have had him.

Page. Why, this is your own folly. Did not 212 I tell you how you should know my daughter by her garments?

Slen. I went to her in white, and cried, 'mum,' and she cried 'budget,' as Anne and I 216 had appointed; and yet it was not Anne, but a postmaster's boy.

[*Eva.* Jeshu! Master Slender, cannot you see put marry poys? 220

Page. O I am vexed at heart: what shall I do?]

Mrs. Page. Good George, be not angry: I knew of your purpose; turned my daughter into 224 green; and, indeed, she is now with the doctor at the deanery, and there married.

[*Enter Caius.*]

Caius. Vere is Mistress Page? By gar, I am cozened: I ha' married *un garçon*, a boy; *un* 228 *paysan*, by gar, a boy; it is not Anne Page: by gar, I am cozened.

Mrs. Page. Why, did you not take her in green?

Caius. Ay, by gar, and 'tis a boy: by gar, I'll 232 raise all Windsor. [*Exit.*]

Ford. This is strange. Who hath got the right Anne?

Page. My heart misgives me: here comes 236 Master Fenton.

[*Enter Fenton and Anne Page.*]

How now, Master Fenton!

Anne. Pardon, good father! good my mother, pardon! 240

Page. Now, mistress, how chance you went
not with Master Slender?

Mrs. Page. Why went you not with Master
Doctor, maid? 244

Fent. You do amaze her: hear the truth of it.
You would have married her most shamefully,
Where there was no proportion held in love.
The truth is, she and I, long since contracted, 248
Are now so sure that nothing can dissolve us.
The offence is holy that she hath committed,
And this deceit loses the name of craft,
Of disobedience, or unduteous title, 252
Since therein she doth evitate and shun
A thousand irreligious cursed hours,
Which forced marriage would have brought upon her.

Ford. Stand not amaz'd: here is no remedy: 256
In love the heavens themselves do guide the state:
Money buys lands, and wives are sold by fate.

Fal. I am glad, though you have ta'en a
special stand to strike at me, that your arrow 260
hath glanced.

Page. Well, what remedy?—Fenton, heaven give
thee joy!
What cannot be eschew'd must be embrac'd.

Fal. When night dogs run all sorts of deer are
chas'd. 264

Mrs. Page. Well, I will muse no further. Master
Fenton,
Heaven give you many, many merry days!
Good husband, let us every one go home,
And laugh this sport o'er by a country fire; 268
Sir John and all.

---

248 contracted: *betrothed*   253 evitate: *avoid*
260 stand: *place from which to shoot*   265 muse: *complain*

Ford.   Let it be so. Sir John,
To Master Brook you yet shall hold your word;
For he to-night shall lie with Mistress Ford. *Exeunt.*

FINIS.

NOTES

I. i. S. d. At the head of each scene of this play in the Folio of 1623 is prefixed a list of all the characters who appear during the scene. Except for these lists, and the *exeunt* at the close of each scene, the Folio is practically without stage-directions. It has been suggested that whoever prepared the play for the Folio was probably influenced by the 'classical method' of dividing plays into scenes, followed in the volume of Ben Jonson's plays published in 1616. By this method a new scene begins every time there is a change of actors on the stage. Thus the exit or entrance of a character marks the beginning of a new scene, and to each scene is prefixed a list of the actors who are actually on the stage during its course.

I. i. 2. *Star-chamber matter.* The Star Chamber was a court deriving its name from the *'chambre des estoiles'* at Westminster, where it sat, beginning with the reign of Edward III. It was proverbially harsh and arbitrary.

I. i. 6. *coram.* Slender is confusing the Latin words *quorum* and *coram*. *Quorum* was the first word of a clause in the commission which named justices, and so came to be a title of certain justices. *Coram* was the first word Shallow would use as justice, in attestation of the legal documents he speaks of in lines 10 and 11: *'Coram me Roberto Shallow, armigero,'* i.e., 'before me Robert Shallow, Esquire.'

I. i. 7, 8. *cust-alorum . . . rato-lorum.* Blunders for *Custos Rotulorum,* Keeper of the Rolls, the principal justice of the peace of a county.

I. i. 16. *luces.* This is evidently a hit at the Warwickshire gentleman, Sir Thomas Lucy of Charlecote, whose game Shakespeare poached while a youth at

Stratford. His arms were 'three luces hauriant argent.' Cf. Appendix B.

I. i. 22, 23. An obscure passage. 'May not the whole point of the matter lie in Shallow's use of the word "salt," the heraldic term used especially for vermin? If so, "salt fish"="leaping louse," with a quibble on "salt" as opposed to "fresh fish." There is a further allusion to the predilection of vermin for "old coats," used quibblingly in the sense of "coats of arms"' (Gollancz).

I. i. 24. *quarter.* In heraldry, to combine the arms of another family with one's own by placing them in one of the four compartments of the shield.

I. i. 93. *Cotsall.* The Cotswolds, a hilly region in Gloucestershire, celebrated for the 'Cotswold games,' where coursing and other rural sports flourished.

I. i. 130-132. Here and elsewhere, passages of the text found in the Quarto of 1602, but not in the Folio, are marked by square brackets.

I. i. 133. *Banbury Cheese.* Proverbially thin, 'nothing but paring.' Bardolph is ridiculing Slender's leanness.

I. i. 135. *Mephistophilus.* The evil spirit attendant upon the hero in Marlowe's tragedy, *Doctor Faustus* (1588).

I. i. 137. *Slice.* Either Nym is still ridiculing Slender's thinness, or he is using the word in its slang sense, meaning to cut, whether to cut with a sword, or 'cut and run.'

I. i. 138. *humour.* According to medieval physiology there were four chief 'humours' (or fluids) in the human body—blood, phlegm, choler and black bile. The relative proportion of these determined whether a person's temperament were sanguine, phlegmatic, choleric or melancholy. In Shakespeare's time 'humour' was the most overworked word in the language, 'racked and tortured with constant abuse,' as Ben Jonson said. It is a favorite with Nym and Pistol.

I. i. 161. *Edward shovel-boards.* Shilling pieces coined in the reign of Edward VI (1547-1553), commonly used in a game which consisted in pushing coins toward a mark. They were sufficiently rare to bring a premium in Shakespeare's day.

I. i. 172, 173. *run ... humour.* 'If you say I am a thief' (Steevens). Nuthook was the slang for constable.

I. i. 179. *Scarlet and John.* Two of Robin Hood's men. Falstaff is ridiculing Bardolph's red face.

I. i. 185. *careires.* A term used to designate galloping a horse at full speed, backward and forward. Probably Bardolph's 'conclusions pass'd the careires' meant 'the words ran high, at full gallop.' Commentators have been as much puzzled by it as is Slender.

I. i. 206. *Book of Songs and Sonnets.* 'Songes and Sonnets, written by the Right Honourable Lord Henry Howard, late Earle of Surrey, and others,' printed in 1557, and very popular during the reign of Queen Elizabeth.

I. i. 310. *Sackerson.* A famous bear exhibited at Paris Garden in Southwark.

I. iii. 9, 10. *Keisar, and Pheezar.* Keisar is another form of Cæsar, the general term for emperor. Pheezar is probably from 'pheeze,' to beat.

I. iii. 14. *froth and lime.* The host calls for an immediate exhibition of Bardolph's abilities as a tapster. Frothing a pot of beer made it appear fuller than it really was; mixing lime with the sack made it sparkle in the glass.

I. iii. 21. Pistol's line is 'a parody on a line taken from one of the old bombast plays' (Steevens).

I. iii. 54. *anchor . . . deep.* 'The scheme for debauching Ford's wife is deep.'

I. iii. 74. *Guiana.* In 1596 Sir Walter Raleigh returned from an expedition to South America and published a book entitled 'The Discoverie of the Large, Rich, and Bewtiful Empyre of Guiana, with a relation of the great and golden Citie of Manoa, which the Spaniards call El Dorado.'

I. iii. 75. *'cheator.* An officer appointed to look after the King's escheats (i.e., properties which fell to a lord by forfeit or fine). He would have abundant opportunity of defrauding people of their estates, hence Falstaff's pun.

I. iii. 81. *Sir Pandarus.* The go-between in the story of Troilus and Cressida. Pistol makes him a knight.

I. iii. 91. *French thrift.* 'An economy then practised in France of making a single page serve in lieu of a train of attendants' (Clarke).

I. iii. 92. *gourd and fullam.* Gourds were hollow dice; fullams were dice loaded at one corner.

I. iv. 23. *Cain-coloured.* 'In old pictures and tapestries Cain and Judas were always represented as having yellow beards, or what we now call sandy-coloured' (Hudson).

I. iv. 131. *An fool's-head.* Mistress Quickly is punning on 'Anne' and 'an' with reference to Caius' speech in line 129.

II. i. 20. *Herod of Jewry.* Herod was the arch-villain in the old mystery plays.

II. i. 23. *Flemish drunkard.* The Flemish were notorious for their intemperance.

II. i. 52. *hack.* This word is a puzzle. 'Grow cheap,' 'kick,' 'deny,' and 'do mischief' are some of the meanings that have been suggested for it. It occurs again in the play, IV. i. 69. Whatever the

exact meaning, the general sense is clearly that
Mrs. Page does not set a high value upon knighthood.

II. i. 61, 62. *disposition would have gone to the
truth of his words.* That is, his character would
have been in accordance with his speech.

II. i. 64. *Green Sleeves.* An old ballad-tune,
usually sung with vulgar words, popular 'from the
time of Elizabeth to the present day.'

II. i. 120. *Actæon . . . Ringwood.* Actæon was a
hunter in classical mythology, who accidentally saw
Diana bathing, and was transformed by her into a
stag. He was then slain by his dogs. Like him
Ford will have 'horns' (the symbol of a cuckold, or
deceived husband) if Falstaff's plans succeed.
Ringwood was a typical dog's name.

II. i. 125. *cuckoo-birds.* The cuckoo's note was
supposed to foretell cuckoldom. Cf. *Love's Labour's
Lost,* V. ii. 908,

> 'The cuckoo then on every tree
> Mocks married men,' etc.

II. i. 147. *Cataian.* Often used as a term of re-
proach. From Cataia, or Cathay, the old name for
China.

II. i. 201. *Cavaliero-justice.* The host is be-
stowing an additional title on Justice Shallow.
Cavaliero meant a gentleman trained in arms; hence
a gallant.

II. i. 202, 203. *Good even and twenty.* 'Good
evening and twenty of 'em!'

II. ii. 4. *equipage.* Pistol may mean 'I'll pay
you in commodities,' i.e., swords, bucklers, etc.; or
(as Greg suggests) the sense may be 'I will return
the money to you in all fairness' (equity).

II. ii. 6. *countenance.* Falstaff means he had gone
surety for Pistol's borrowings. He is punning on

the two meanings of countenance: (1) face, and (2) patronage.

II. ii. 13. *handle.* Fans were often set in handles of gold and silver.

II. ii. 20. *Pickt-hatch.* A district of ill-repute in London, the houses having hatches or half-doors guarded with spikes to prevent marauders from 'leaping the hatch.' (Cf. *King Lear,* III. vi. 76.)

II. ii. 144. *fights.* A kind of screen used during naval engagements to protect the crew of a vessel.

II. ii. 145. *my prize.* Perhaps an intimation of the fate of Mistress Quickly. In *Henry V* we find Pistol has married her.

II. ii. 159. *Brooks.* Throughout the play as printed in the Folio, Ford's assumed name is Broome. Falstaff's pun here, and the authority of the two Quartos, have led modern editors to follow Pope in reading Brook throughout the play. Wright suggests the name may have been altered at the instance of someone named Brook, who had influence with the actors or their patron.

II. ii. 220, 221. Cf. Ben Jonson's

"Follow a shadow, it still flies you;
    Seem to fly it, it will pursue:
So court a mistress, she denies you;
    Let her alone, she will court you."

II. ii. 312, 313. *stand under the adoption of abominable terms.* Have to submit to being called by vile names.

II. iii. 26, 27. *punto . . . montant.* The punto was a blow with the point of the sword, the stock or stoccado (cf. II. i. 233) a thrust, the reverse a backhand stroke, and the montant an upward blow.

II. iii. 30. *heart of elder.* 'In contradistinction to "heart of oak," elder wood having nothing but soft pith at heart' (Clarke). *Stale.* Slang term for physician. The word means urine, and alludes to the practice of examining patients' water in diagnosing cases.

II. iii. 77. *Frogmore.* Now best known as the site of the mansion in Little Park, Windsor, built for the late King Edward VII while Prince of Wales.

II. iii. 91, 92. *Cried game.* 'The sport is arranged and proclaimed' (Hart). The phrase is from bear-baiting.

III. i. 5. *pittie-ward.* Towards the Petty or Little Park, as distinguished from the Windsor Great Park.

III. i. 17-26. Stanzas from a popular song by Christopher Marlowe. In line 24 Sir Hugh substi-tutes for one of Marlowe's lines a line from a metrical version of Psalm 137.

III. i. 46, 47. *doublet and hose.* The ordinary men's dress in Elizabethan times was the doublet, a close-fitting garment extending to the hips, and hose. Out of doors, and in cold weather a cloak or *gown* (line 34) was worn outside this. The latter still survives in the academic gown.

III. ii. 47. *cry aim.* Archers when about to shoot were encouraged by cries of 'Aim!'

III. ii. 77. *prince and Poins.* This is a reference to the adventures of Falstaff in *Henry IV*, where he is the associate of Prince Hal and his companions.

III. ii. 94. *pipe-wine.* There is a pun here upon pipe in its double sense of a cask and a musical instrument. It is suggested by Falstaff's mention in line 92, of canary, which was the name of a lively dance, as well as a sort of wine.

III. iii. 15. *Datchet-mead.* An open meadow by the river, where clothes were washed out of doors as they are in France to-day. The village of Datchet is two miles east of Windsor, on the left bank of the Thames.

III. iii. 45. Falstaff is quoting the opening line of

the second song of **Sir Philip Sidney's** *Astrophel and Stella,* which begins:

> 'Have I caught my heavenly jewel
>   Teaching sleepe most faire to be?'

III. iii. 69, 70. *Fortune thy foe.* An allusion to a popular old song beginning 'Fortune my foe, why dost thou frown on me?'

III. iii. 79. *Bucklersbury.* A street off Cheapside in London, inhabited by herbalists, who sold all sorts of simples or medicinal herbs.

III. iii. 175. *uncape.* Ford is here using the language of the hunting-field. 'The collar of the grayhound was sometimes called his cape; a term equally applicable to the couple (or leash) of the running hound' (Madden). Hence to uncape would mean to uncouple, or set free, the hounds.

III. iii. 245. *a-birding.* Birding was hawking with a sparrow hawk. Page's hawk is especially trained 'for the bush'; that is he flies at small birds which take refuge in a bush, where they can be shot.

III. iv. 24. *a shaft or a bolt.* A shaft was a long slender arrow, a bolt a short thick one. Slender's whole phrase means 'I'll do it one way or another.'

III. v. 115. *bilbo.* The swords of Bilbao, in Spain, were noted for the temper and elasticity of their blades. The test of a good sword was that it could be bent into a circle.

IV. i. 51. *Hang-hog . . . bacon.* Probably suggested by an anecdote of Sir Nicholas Bacon. A prisoner named Hog had been condemned to death and prayed for mercy on the ground of kindred. 'Ay,' replied the judge, 'but you and I cannot be of kindred unless you be hanged, for Hog is not Bacon till it be well hanged.'

IV. ii. 79, 80. *fat woman of Brainford.* 'The

witch of Brentford,' a well-known personage of Shakespeare's day, kept a tavern at Brentford, a town on the Thames about twelve miles directly east of Windsor. In the 1602 Quarto of *The Merry Wives,* and in Dekker and Webster's *Westward Ho!* she is spoken of as 'Gillian of Brainford.'

IV. ii. 189. *figure.* To 'work by the figure' meant to operate on a wax effigy of a person for the purpose of enchantment.

IV. ii. 229. *fine and recovery.* The means by which an estate tail was converted into a fee simple, so that the owner might dispose of it as he wished.

IV. iii. 1. *The Germans.* Perhaps an allusion to the visit to Windsor in 1592 of Count Frederick of Mompelgard, afterwards Duke of Wurtemberg and Teck (cf. IV. v. 90). In the text of the 1602 edition of the play there is evidently a reference to his title in the lines:

> There is three sorts of cosen garmombles
> Is cosen all the Hosts of Maidenhead and Readings.

Post horses were furnished him gratis during his stay, through a pass of Lord Howard.

IV. iv. 77. *Eton.* Town in Buckinghamshire across the Thames from Windsor, famous for the school founded there in 1440 by Henry VI.

IV. v. 29. *mussel-shell.* 'He calls poor Simple mussel-shell because he stands with his mouth open' (Johnson).

IV. v. 71. *Doctor Faustuses.* Faustus was the famous mediæval scholar who obtained magic power for twenty-four years by selling his soul to the devil. He is the hero of Marlowe's tragedy of *Doctor Faustus.*

IV. v. 79. *cozen-germans.* A pun on cousin-german, relative, and cozening, or cheating, Germans.

IV. v. 104. *crest-fallen as a dried pear.* 'Pears when they are dried become flat, and lose the erect and oblong form that distinguishes them from apples' (Steevens).

V. i. 25. *life is a shuttle.* Falstaff is thinking of Job 7. 6: 'My days are swifter than a weaver's shuttle, and are spent without hope.'

V. ii. 6, 7. *mum . . . budget.* 'To play mum-budget' was 'to be tongue-tyed, to say never a word.'

V. v. 4. *Europa.* The sister of Cadmus, who was carried off by Jove in the shape of a bull. Her story is told by Ovid, *Metamorphoses,* ii. 833 ff.

V. v. 7. *Leda.* Courted by Jupiter in the shape of a swan. The story is given in the *Odyssey,* Book xi, and in Ovid's *Metamorphoses* vi. 109 ff.

V. v. 30. *woodman.* Falstaff is priding himself on his knowledge of the rules for cutting up and apportioning a buck.

V. v. 32. *child of conscience.* Cupid is conscientious, and will requite him for his past misfortunes.

V. v. 45. *orphan heirs.* Fairies were believed to be of spontaneous birth, and so were 'created orphans by fate.'

V. v. 57. 'Exalt her imagination by pleasant dreams.'

V. v. 67. *chairs of order.* The stalls in St. George's Chapel at Windsor assigned to the Knights of the Garter, an order of Knighthood, founded about 1347 by Edward III (1327-1377). The emblem of the order is a blue garter with the motto *'Honi soit qui mal y pense.'*

V. v. 113. *yokes.* Alluding to the antlers on Falstaff's head, which bore some resemblance to the projections on the top of ox-yokes.

V. v. 176, 177. *Ignorance . . . me.* 'Ignorance has sounded me,' or 'got to the bottom of me.'

APPENDIX A

SOURCES OF THE PLAY

The Merry Wives of Windsor ranks next after *Love's Labour's Lost, A Midsummer Night's Dream,* and *The Tempest* among Shakespeare's plays, as owing least to any definite sources for its plot. It is a comedy of contemporary manners, and most of its details seem to be original with Shakespeare.

There are two elements in the plot for which parallels can be found in contemporary English and Italian literature. The first of these is the incident of the women who discover that one gallant is courting them simultaneously, and their luring him on successively, only to make a laughingstock of him in the end. A story of this sort which Shakespeare may have seen is found in William Painter's *Palace of Pleasure,* published at London in 1566. The 49th tale in Painter's first volume is a free adaptation of an Italian story told by Straparola and by Ser Giovanni Fiorentino, whose novels were printed in Italy about 1550. In Painter's story, Philenio Sisterno, a scholar of Bologna, meets three ladies at a ball, and professes his devotion to each in turn. The ladies' discovery of his deceit and their determination to make a mockery of him have some slight resemblance to the story of Mrs. Ford and Mrs. Page and their revenge on Falstaff.

'Esmerentiana, the wife of Seignior Lamberto, not for any euill, but in sporting wise said vnto her companions: "Gentlewomen, I have gotten this night in daucing, a curteous louer, a very faire Gentleman, and of so good behauiour as any one in the world": and from point to point, (she) rehearsed vnto them all that he had said. Which Panthemia and Sim-

phorosia vnderstanding, answered, that the like had
chaunced vnto them, and they departed not from
the feaste before eche of them knewe him that was
their louer: whereby they perceiued that his woordes
proceded not of faithful Loue, but rather of follie and
dissimulation, and they separated not from thence
vntill all three with one accorde, had conspired
every one to give him mocke.' Each of the ladies then
sends Philenio an invitation to visit her and each tricks
him when he comes to her house. Esmerentiana's
husband returns unexpectedly, and she claps Philenio
into a hiding-place which she had filled with 'fagots
of sharp thorns.' Panthemia leads him into a closet,
and a loose board in the floor precipitates him into an
outhouse, where he spends a miserable night. Sim-
phorosia gives him drugged wine, which he drinks all
unsuspecting. Her servants then strip him and fling
him into the street, where he lies unconscious until
morning.

Another element in Shakespeare's plot, which may
have been suggested by several contemporary stories,
is that of the lover who unwittingly confides his plans
to the jealous husband of his lady. This theme is
found in the *Tale of the two lovers of Pisa* in Tarl-
ton's *Newes out of Purgatorie,* a collection of stories
published in 1590. In this tale, Mutio, an old doctor
of Pisa, discovers that Lionello is courting Margaret,
the beautiful woman he has just married. Lionello
informs his friend of his plans for meeting Margaret,
so Mutio is able to break in upon them each time.
Margaret is quick of wit, and manages to conceal her
lover—once in a 'dry-vat' full of feathers; again
'between two ceilings of a chamber,' and finally in an
old chest where valuable papers are stored. This time
Mutio is sure Lionello is in the house, so he sets fire
to the room, and Margaret saves her lover by bidding
the servants carry out the chest.

Similar stories by Straparola and Ser Giovanni Fiorentino have interesting parallels to Mrs. Ford's trick of concealing Falstaff in the buck-basket. In these stories the wife makes use of 'a chest with clothes in front,' or 'a heap of wet clothes from the wash' for hiding her lover. But it is doubtful if English translations of them were available at the time *The Merry Wives* was written. A translation of one of them (printed in 1632) describes the husband in words that might apply to Shakespeare's Ford, as 'a person naturally inclin'd to jealousy (a passion extraordinarily reigning in Italy).' Recent scholars have been interested in elements in the play that may be derived from ancient Roman comedy.

Except for such details as may be drawn from these sources, *The Merry Wives of Windsor* is of Shakespeare's own invention. It is the only one of his plays which deals exclusively with English country society.

APPENDIX B

The History of the Play

The Merry Wives of Windsor was entered on the Stationers' Register on January 18, 1602. It was published the same year as a small Quarto, which was reprinted in 1619. The text of both is very corrupt. Comparison of them with the text of the Folio, published in 1623, seems to indicate that the publisher of the Quarto secured his version of the play by taking it down as best he could from the mouths of the players, perhaps with some assistance from one of them.

The play was probably written in 1599. In the

epilogue to the *Second Part of Henry IV* (produced about 1598), Shakespeare had written: 'If you be not too much cloy'd with fat meat, our humble author will continue the story with Sir John in it . . . where for anything I know Falstaff shall die of a sweat, unless a' be killed already with your hard opinions.' *The Merry Wives* seems to offer the promised continuation of Sir John's adventures.

Two interesting traditions have long been current about the play. The first of these is that it was written at the command of Queen Elizabeth, and in a period of fourteen days. John Dennis, writing in 1702, says of the play: 'I know very well that it hath pleased one of the greatest queens that ever was in the world. . . . This comedy was written at her command, and by her direction, and she was so eager to see it acted that she commanded it to be finished in fourteen days; and was afterwards, as tradition tells us, very well pleased at the representation.' Rowe repeated the story in his *Life of Shakespeare*, adding of Queen Elizabeth: 'She was so well pleased with that admirable character of Falstaff in the two parts of *Henry the Fourth*, that she commanded him to continue it for one play more, and to show him in love. This is said to be the occasion of his writing *The Merry Wives of Windsor*. How well she was obeyed, the play itself is an admirable proof.'

The other tradition is that in Justice Shallow, Shakespeare is satirizing Sir Thomas Lucy of Charlecote, near Stratford, who had prosecuted him in his youth for poaching. According to a note by Archdeacon Davies, written probably between 1688 and 1707, Shakespeare was 'much given to all un-luckinesse in stealing venison and Rabbits particu-larly from Sr. Lucy, . . . but his reveng is so great that he is his Justice Clodpate, and calls him a great man and that in allusion to his name bore three lowses rampant for his Arms.' Rowe, in 1709, adds to this: 'Amongst other extravagancies, in *The Merry Wives of Windsor* he has made him a deer-stealer, that he might at the same time remember his Warwickshire prosecutor under the name of Justice Shallow; he has given him very near the same coat of arms which Dugdale, in his Antiquities of that county, describes for a family there, and makes the Welsh parson descant very pleasantly upon them.'

Of the earliest performances of the play we know from the title-page of the 1602 Quarto that it was 'divers times acted, both before her Majesty and elsewhere.' Shakespeare's company presented it at Whitehall before King James during the winter of 1604-1605; and another court performance occurred in 1612-1613. The play was presented before Charles I also; for in the records of Sir Henry Herbert is the entry: 'before the king and queene this yeare of our Lord 1638. . . . At the Cocpit the 15th of November. The merry wifes of winser.'

Of the actors in these productions we know nothing definite. John Heminge, a member of Shakespeare's company and one of editors of the 1623 Folio, is said to have been the original Falstaff; and after the Restoration John Lowen (1576-1659) was remembered as having excelled in the part 'before the wars.'

The Merry Wives was one of the first plays revived after the Commonwealth. On December 5, 1660, Pepys records seeing it with 'the humours of the country gentlemen and the French doctor very well done, but the rest but very poorly, and Sir J. Falstaffe as bad as any.' In 1661 he went again to the theatre 'such is the power of the Devil over me . . . and saw the Merry Wives ill done.' And in 1667 yet another production of the play 'did not please me at all in no part.'

When the Drury Lane Theatre opened in 1663

The Merry Wives was one of the productions which 'being well performed were very satisfactory to the town'; and forty years later John Dennis still remembered Wintersel's success as Falstaff 'in King Charles the Second's reign.'

In 1702 Dennis produced an adaptation of *The Merry Wives* under the title of *The Comical Gallant, or the Amours of Sir John Falstaff*. Falstaff's beating at the end of the play is shifted to Ford, to punish him for his jealousy, and Sir John is spared the humiliation of appearing in women's clothes, but he has a far more degrading part to play when he is bullied by Mrs. Page, disguised as a roistering captain. Dennis' piece 'was received but coldly,' and the original play was soon afterward successfully revived by Betterton, with Mrs. Bracegirdle, and later Peg Woffington, in the rôle of Mrs. Ford.

During the eighteenth century the part of Falstaff was ably interpreted by Quin, Henderson, and Cooke. Horace Walpole wrote on hearing of Quin's death, 'Pray, who is to give an idea of Falstaff, now Quin is dead?' John Henderson (1747-1785) won great applause in the part. Rogers in his table-talk says 'his Hamlet and his Falstaff were equally good.' Kemble revised the play in 1797, and successfully produced his version a few years later, playing Ford to the Falstaff of George Frederick Cooke. Cooke later visited the United States, where he died in 1811. *The Merry Wives* had already been produced in this country in 1770, at the Southwark Theatre in Philadelphia.

During the nineteenth century the play has been a favorite source for librettos for operas. In 1824 Frederick Reynolds was 'censured as an interpolator, for converting Shakespeare's plays into operas'; but his production of the *Merry Wives* ran for thirty-two performances at Drury Lane, and was a great success.

In 1838 Balfe's opera, *Falstaff,* with an Italian libretto by Maggioni, was produced at London. Nine years later a German version, *Die lustigen Weiber von Windsor,* with music by Nicolai, was given in Berlin. Nicolai's work was soon afterwards produced in Paris with some amusingly Gallic touches— Fenton is transformed into a young poet; Caius becomes a bullying captain; and Anne Page's character suffers by being made deceitful and dishonest. Perhaps to balance these French features *Rule Britannia* was introduced into a chorus toward the end of the piece. The greatest of the operatic versions of the play is Verdi's *Falstaff* (1893).

During all this time the original comedy has maintained its popularity on the stage. Among innumerable modern productions may be mentioned that at the New Theatre in New York (1910), and those of Sir Herbert Tree, who 'made Falstaff such a merry rogue that you forgot his cowardice and his grossness in laughing at his conceit and his mock bravery.' Tree's productions of the play in England and America were elaborately mounted, and generally accompanied by the music for the lyrics composed by Arthur Sullivan in 1874. The play is a favorite for amateur performances. It was presented by the Yale Dramatic Association in 1909.

APPENDIX C

The Text of the Present Edition

The text of the present volume is, by permission of the Oxford University Press, that of the Oxford Shakespeare, edited by the late W. J. Craig, except for the following deviations:

1. In accordance with the plan of this series, the

stage-directions of the First Folio have been preserved
so far as possible. Modern additions to these are
enclosed in square brackets, and passages of the text
found only in the Quarto are similarly marked.

2. A few unimportant changes have been made in
punctuation and the spelling of a few words has been
normalized, as anything for any thing, Gloucester,
Gloucestershire for Gloster, Glostershire, lantern for
lanthorn, mussel-shell for muscle-shell, œillades for
œilliades, Poins for Pointz, till for 'till, villainy, villainous for villany, villanous, warlike for war-like.

3. The following changes in punctuation or word-
ing have been made, all of them being reversions to
the readings of the Folio. The readings of the
present edition precede the colon and Craig's follow
in each case:

I. iv. 23	Cain-coloured: cane-coloured
	(Folio Caine-colourd)
II. i. 104	look where: look, where
II. ii. 20	Pickt-hatch: Picht-hatch
II. iii. 91, 92	Cried game;: Cried I aim?
	(Folio Cride-game,)
III. i. 99	Gaul: Guallia
	(Folio Gaule)
III. iii. 114	in Windsor: of Windsor
III. v. 69	sped: how sped
III. v. 157	one: me
IV. i. 12	let: get
IV. i. 51	Hang-hog: Hang hog
IV. i. 71	horum;: horum?
IV. i. 74	of: and
IV. ii. 22	lines: lunes
IV. ii. 139	Mistress Ford; Mistress Ford,: Mistress Ford,
IV. ii. 208	his: her
IV. v. 31	master: Master
IV. v. 55	sir: like: Sir Tike;
IV. vi. 17	scene: scare
V. iii. 11	heart-break: heart break
	(Folio hearte-break)
V. v. 57	Raise: Rein
V. v. 59	as: that

APPENDIX D

Suggestions for Collateral Reading

W. H. Ainsworth: *Windsor Castle* (1843).

Mary Cowden Clarke: 'The Merry Maids of Windsor' in *The Girlhood of Shakespeare's Heroines* (1850-1882). (In vol. i of the Everyman's Library ed.)

D. H. Madden: *The Diary of Master William Silence* (1897).

W. W. Greg: *Shakespeare's Merry Wives of Windsor*. (A reprint of the 1602 Quarto.) (Clarendon Press, 1910.)

John Masefield in *Shakespeare* (1911). (Home University Library.)

R. S. Forsythe: *A Plautine Source of "The Merry Wives of Windsor."* Modern Philology, December, 1920.

INDEX OF WORDS GLOSSED

(Figures in full-faced type refer to page-numbers)